• CELEBRATING HOLIDAYS & FESTIVALS AROUND THE WORLD •

Carnival

Christmas & Hanukkah

Easter, Passover & Festivals of Hope

Halloween & Remembrances of the Dead

Independence Days

Lent, Yom Kippur & Days of Repentance

Marking the Religious New Year

Ramadan

Ringing in the Western & Chinese New Year

Thanksgiving & Other Festivals of the Harvest

KEY ICONS TO LOOK FOR:

 Words to understand: These words with their easy-to-understand definitions will increase the reader's understanding of the text while building vocabulary skills.

 Sidebars: This boxed material within the main text allows readers to build knowledge, gain insights, explore possibilities, and broaden their perspectives by weaving together additional information to provide realistic and holistic perspectives.

 Educational Videos: Readers can view videos by scanning our QR codes, providing them with additional educational content to supplement the text. Examples include news coverage, moments in history, speeches, iconic sports moments and much more!

 Text-dependent Questions: These questions send the reader back to the text for more careful attention to the evidence presented there.

 Research projects: Readers are pointed toward areas of further inquiry connected to each chapter. Suggestions are provided for projects that encourage deeper research and analysis.

 Series glossary of key terms: This back-of-the book glossary contains terminology used throughout this series. Words found here increase the reader's ability to read and comprehend higher-level books and articles in this field.

Halloween &
Remembrances of the Dead

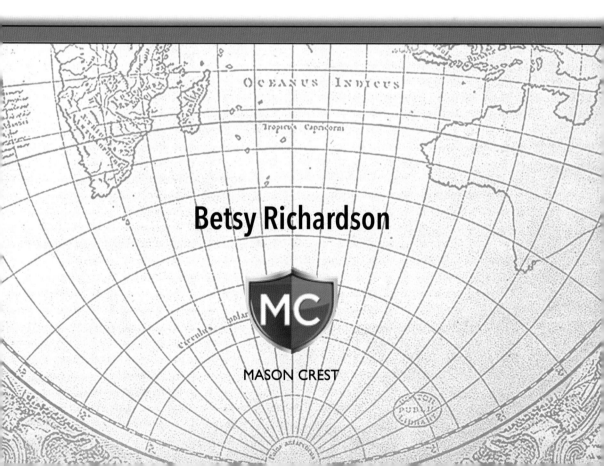

Betsy Richardson

MASON CREST

Mason Crest
450 Parkway Drive, Suite D Broomall, PA 19008
www.masoncrest.com

Copyright © 2019 by Mason Crest, an imprint of National Highlights, Inc. All rights reserved. No part of this publication may be reproduced or transmitted in any form or by any means, electronic or mechanical, including photocopying, recording, taping, or any information storage and retrieval system, without permission in writing from the publisher.

Printed in the United States of America
First printing
9 8 7 6 5 4 3 2 1

Series ISBN: 978-1-4222-4143-1
Hardcover ISBN: 978-1-4222-4147-9

Library of Congress Cataloging-in-Publication Data is available on file.

Developed and Produced by Print Matters Productions, Inc. (www.printmattersinc.com)
Cover and Interior Design by Lori S Malkin Design LLC

CONTENTS

Celebrating Holidays & Festivals Around the World

Holidays mark time. They occupy a space outside of ordinary events and give shape and meaning to our everyday existence. They also remind us of the passage of time as we reflect on Christmases, Passovers, or Ramadans past. Throughout human history, nations and peoples have marked their calendars with special days to celebrate, commemorate, and memorialize. We set aside times to reflect on the past and future, to rest and renew physically and spiritually, and to simply have fun.

In English we call these extraordinary moments "holidays," a contraction of the term "holy day." Sometimes holidays are truly holy days–the Sabbath, Easter, or Eid al-Fitr, for example–but they can also be nonreligious occasions that serve political purposes, address the social needs of communities and individuals, or focus on regional customs and games.

This series explores the meanings and celebrations of holidays across religions and cultures around the world. It groups the holidays into volumes according to theme (such as *Lent, Yom Kippur & Days of Repentance*; *Thanksgiving & Other Festivals of the Harvest*; *Independence Days*; *Easter, Passover & Festivals of Hope*; *Ringing in the Western & Chinese New Year*; *Marking the Religious New Year*; *Carnival*; *Ramadan*; and *Halloween & Remembrances of the Dead*) or by their common human experience due to their closeness on the calendar (such as *Christmas & Hanukkah*). Each volume introduces readers to the origins, history, and common practices associated with the holidays before embarking on a worldwide tour that shows the regional variations and distinctive celebrations within specific countries. The reader will learn how these holidays started, what they mean to the people who celebrate them, and how different cultures celebrate them.

▲ A Halloween decoration display in New Mexico.

These volumes have an international focus, and thus readers will be able to learn about diversity both at home and throughout the world. We can learn a great deal about a people or nation by the holidays they celebrate. We can also learn from holidays how cultures and religions have interacted and mingled over time. We see in celebrations not just the past through tradition, but the principles and traits that people embrace and value today.

The Celebrating Holidays & Festivals Around the World series surveys this rich and varied festive terrain. Its 10 volumes show the distinct ways that people all over the world infuse ordinary life with meaning, purpose, or joy. The series cannot be all-inclusive or the last word on so vast a subject, but it offers a vital first step for those eager to learn more about the diverse, fascinating, and vibrant cultures of the world, through the festivities that give expression, order, and meaning to their lives.

INTRODUCTION

Halloween & Remembrances of the Dead

Death is a natural and inevitable part of the human experience. As the human brain became more developed, humankind came to realize that every living thing must eventually die. Even after accepting this truth, however, human beings have found it difficult to part with loved ones. When family members or friends die, people feel the need to set aside a special time to honor and remember them. In response to this desire, most civilizations, whether ancient or modern, have devoted a special holiday to honoring the dead. Moreover, many cultures have created holidays dedicated to death itself, perhaps as a way of coming to terms with this unavoidable end that comes to all living beings.

Many Western countries share similar practices for celebrating the dead. For example, people in the United States, Ireland, the United Kingdom, France, and Iceland all celebrate a holiday called Halloween in some way. Recently this holiday has become popular with children in other European countries as well. Today Halloween is highly commercialized and thus retains little spiritual significance. Nevertheless, it originated as a holiday dedicated to death. Some celebrations similar to Halloween were originally dedicated not to death itself but to loved ones who have died. One such holiday is Day of the Dead, which is celebrated in many countries in Latin America, including Mexico, Guatemala, and El Salvador. Because much of Latin America was colonized by the Spanish, there is a strong link between Day of the Dead and the Christian holidays All Saints' Day, All Souls' Day, and the Soul Saturday Radonitsa, which are dedicated to deceased saints and ancestors. When All Saints' Day and All Souls' Day were introduced and established as holidays in the new Spanish colonies, the indigenous people had their own holidays dedicated to death and did not accept the Spanish traditions. Over time, however, the

Spanish and indigenous traditions surrounding the holidays melded to form new customs. Today's Day of the Dead celebrations still show elements of both the indigenous observances as well as All Saints' Day and All Souls' Day. In addition, some of the popular customs of Halloween have influenced these celebrations. The resulting holiday celebrates death in general while also honoring an individual's deceased ancestors.

Some cultures have holidays specifically devoted to honoring deceased relatives. On Tomb Sweeping Day, many people from Asian countries, such as China and Taiwan, go to cemeteries to honor their dead. Families gather at the graves of their loved ones to clean and decorate the gravesites. They prepare food to enjoy together and to offer to the deceased. Also celebrated in Asia is the Ghost Festival. This festival involves elaborate feasts prepared for both the living and the dead. People believe that during this time their deceased ancestors return to the world of the living to enjoy the feasts and to visit with their families.

◀ Revelers dressed as a skeleton for a Day of the Dead celebration in El Salvador on November 1.

1

Origins and Celebrations of Halloween

Mostly celebrated in North America, Halloween is a day children dress in costumes and go door-to-door in their neighborhoods "trick-or-treating" for candy. Homes and offices are decorated and parties are often thrown. Witches and ghosts are popular themes of the day. People also carve pumpkins known as jack-o'-lanterns. While today Halloween is a secular holiday mostly celebrated for fun, many of the traditions found in today's popular Halloween celebrations can be traced back thousands of years through a long series of influences and cultures.

WORDS TO UNDERSTAND

Celts: Indigenous peoples of the British Isles and Galatia.
Druids: Celtic priests and keepers of the community's history.
Folklorists: People who study the cultures, stories, legends, and beliefs of a specific group or culture.

◀ The pre-Christian Celts celebrated Samhain, which is one of the earliest festivals honoring the dead. This costumed performer was part of a modern Samhain-inspired celebration in Edinburgh, Scotland.

■ Origins

SAMHAIN

One of the earliest known examples of a celebration involving the dead is the ancient Celtic festival of Samhain. The **Celts** were a group of people who lived in Europe beginning in the second millennium B.C.E. (between the years 1999 B.C.E. and 1000 B.C.E.), and possibly much earlier.

Carrying iron tools and weapons for conquering other peoples, and traveling on horseback, the Celts spread across much of the European continent and the British Isles. At some point around the fourth century B.C.E. Germanic tribes began to seize control of some areas of Europe formerly under Celtic rule. After that period, the history of the Celtic peoples began to blend with that of the invading tribes. Nevertheless, historians agree that groups of Celts continued to live across Europe well into the first century B.C.E.

The Celtic word *Samhain*, or *Samain*, means "end of summer," and indeed this holiday is believed to have marked the transition from the summer season to autumn and winter, as well as the Celtic new year. Because the Celts lived so long ago, it is difficult for historians to decipher the details surrounding this holiday. As a result, there is much disagreement when it comes to the specific aspects of the celebration of Samhain. What is known, however, is that many of the traditions of Samhain, as well as the date of the holiday, have carried over into the modern celebration of Halloween.

Many believe Samhain was the date every year on which the shepherds brought their flocks in from the pastures and people began preparing for the winter season. Winter was also known as the "lord of death." The Celts believed that on their New Year's Eve, the last day of the month of October, the border between the worlds of the living and the dead opened, allowing the souls of the dead to return to the realm of the living and to the homes they had left behind. These spirits, along with the Celtic gods, were believed to create havoc, harm crops, and play tricks on the living. Some of the common symbols of Halloween, such as witches and goblins, may rise out of these ancient beliefs.

The Celtic people employed many tactics to avoid the malicious intentions of these spirits, including dressing up in hideous disguises made with animal heads and skins so that they might be mistaken for fellow spirits and left alone. They also offered gifts to the gods, often in the form of sweets or animal sacrifices. Often they would leave food on their doorsteps. The Celts hoped these gifts would please the gods and spirits and keep them from interfering in the lives of the living.

Fire also played an important role in the Samhain festival. At night, the Celtic people would gather on hilltops and light large bonfires. One purpose of these fires was to burn the plant waste from harvesting the crops. But the fires were also seen as a way to scare off the evil spirits, and were often stoked further with the bones from animals slaughtered either as food for the winter or as sacrifices to the gods. Some historians also believe people would intentionally put out the everyday fires in the fireplaces of their homes and relight them later from the great bonfires, which they viewed as sacred and as a way to protect themselves over the winter. The idea was that the spiritual power of the bonfire would be transferred to the home fire.

STOKING THE FIRE

Farm animals were often slaughtered during the celebration of Samhain to provide food for the winter months. The bones from these animals were thrown together and burned along with sticks and unused remains of crops, creating a huge bone-fire. Many people believe that as a result of this practice, any large fire came to be known as *bonfire*.

The supernatural nature of this holiday was also believed to allow the Celtic priests, known as **druids**, to see into the future and predict events to come. These holy people were very important to the Celts, and their predictions pertained to individuals as well as to the fortunes of the entire tribe.

◀ Children dressed for Halloween trick-or-treat in the Philippines.

FERALIA AND PARENTALIA

By the first century C.E., the Celts, like many other civilizations, had been conquered by the Roman Empire, whose influence spread across much of what is now the European continent and beyond. With the arrival of the Romans, the old customs of Samhain were replaced by Roman traditions and deities.

One of the Roman festivals was Feralia, the last day in a week-long series of events in the name of the *manen*, the spirits of the dead. The celebration started on February 13 with the festival of Parentalia, which celebrated all the family members who were dead. The commemorations were held in private until the last day, when Feralia took place. On this public holiday people made their way to the graves and left their offerings of remembrance.

The festival took place in February because, according to Roman lore, it was the most unlucky month in the Roman calendar. Romans believed that in February the spirits of the departed would become restless and need appeasing. Because it was the most turbulent period, no one got married or carried on any of their customary business transactions between Parentalia and Feralia.

FUSION OF CUSTOMS

Historians and **folklorists** agree that a fusion of customs probably occurred during the 400 years the Romans ruled the Celts, with the Celtic festival of Samhain merging with the Roman festival of Feralia and also with Pomona. Pomona was a festival celebrating the Roman goddess of the same name who presided over gardens and orchards. Pomona's Latin name, Pomun, means "fruit." Her symbol is the apple, though she is also associated with nuts, grapes, and other fruits. Pomona is often depicted as a maiden with fruit in her arms and a pruning knife in her hand. For the Romans, the apple was a symbol of love and fertility. This was combined with the feeling of divination surrounding Samhain and resulted in an overall aura of romance, magic, and enchantment. The Pomona festival took place around November 1 and 2. One tradition was to bury apples in the ground to provide nourishment for the souls traveling between the two worlds. Another practice was bobbing for apples. To bob apples, a large tub was first filled with water. Apples were floated in the water and contestants tried to retrieve the apples using their teeth alone. According to one legend, the first to take a bite of a bobbing apple using the mouth only would be the first to marry. According to another, if a girl put the apple she bobbed beneath her pillow, she would dream of her future spouse.

CHRISTIANITY

Around the time of its establishment nearly 2,000 years ago, the Roman Catholic Church endeavored to transform pagan local celebrations into Christian holidays. For centuries the Church had designated the observance of All Saints' Day as a day to exalt the saints. Traditionally All Saints' Day was celebrated in May. Because the Celts were reluctant to give up their Samhain end-of-summer celebration, however, the Church blended and fused Samhain with All Saints' Day to evolve what is now known as the Eve of All Saints, Eve of All Hallows, or Hallow Eve, celebrated in the fall. The name eventually became Halloween.

■ Celebrating Halloween

COSTUMES AND TRICK-OR-TREATING

Although children today do not dress up in order to hide from evil spirits, they are unknowingly carrying on a Celtic tradition by wearing costumes. Modern-day Halloween costumes, though not as grotesque as those made of animal heads and skins worn during Samhain, still tend to favor frightening subjects such as monsters, witches, skeletons, ghosts, and beasts. In addition, funny and contemporary costumes, such as cartoon characters, celebrities, objects, superheroes, and politicians, are also popular. Dressed in these costumes children go trick-or-treating. Trick-or-treating

▲ Costumed participants march during a Halloween parade in Kawasaki, Japan.

involves children going door-to-door in costume and asking for sweets. People may give candy, or healthier things such as nuts and fruit. One popular candy to give on Halloween is candy corn, a sweet designed to resemble a kernel of corn (a food traditionally associated with the autumn harvest). The tradition of giving candy stems from when people would offer animal sacrifices and other such gifts to the gods and spirits during Samhain. It is also related to the European practice of souling, an ancient tradition of going house-to-house on November 1. Children would dress up in homemade costumes and roam their neighborhoods offering a blessing or song in exchange for a sweet oatcake known as a *soulcake*. Families who did not respond were punished by harmless pranks.

■ Parties and Contests

Children and their families may congregate at Halloween parties put on by local organizations such as schools, churches, or civic groups. Often these parties will feature a haunted house elaborately filled with scary characters and scenes. Characters surprise families wandering through the houses.

▲ Dressed in Halloween costumes, thousands of people make their way to Belvedere Street in Cole Valley, San Francisco for the annual trick or treating event.

They hide behind the scenery and pounce out unexpectedly, dispensing candy to children as they pass. The parties usually culminate in a costume contest where judges decide which of the children has the best costume in the categories of funniest, scariest, and most original, with prizes going to all the winners. Smaller parties are also often thrown by friends and family members. Both children and adults attend Halloween parties, usually in costume. Halloween decorations are prominent and Halloween "music," such as the sound of squeaking doors, screams, or sinister laughs may accompany the event. Bobbing for apples is also a popular activity.

BONFIRES AND JACK-O'-LANTERNS

During Samhain, young people would venture door-to-door, collecting not only food offerings but also kindling for large fires used to summon the gods. Animal offerings were placed on top of these open fires as a way of winning the gods' favor. Though such offerings are rarely made today, the

◀ A jack-o'-lantern in Tyler, Texas.

JACK-O'-LANTERN AND PEAT

The term *jack-o'-lantern* also refers to an ancient description of the way light looks when it flickers over peat bogs in rural Celtic landscapes.

tradition of the Halloween bonfire continues in many places all around the world. Cities and towns may host large bonfires in various open spaces as an alternative to door-to-door trick-or-treating.

A more controlled use of fire on Halloween occurs with the use of jack-o'-lanterns, or pumpkins hollowed, carved into frightening faces, and illuminated from within by a candle. This jack-o'-lantern custom originated in Ireland with the myth of a man named Jack who, after dying, could not get into either heaven or hell. He was doomed to walk the Earth in search of a final resting place. Before Jack began to walk the Earth, the devil went into hell, picked up a piece of lighted coal, and gave it to him. Jack put the coal into a carved-out turnip and with the aid of that shining light walked from place to place searching for his final resting spot. According to legend, Jack has been roaming the Earth ever since. Jack became known as "Jack of the Lantern," which, over time, became abbreviated to "Jack o'Lantern." People all over Ireland and Scotland began making their own versions of Jack's turnip lantern, sometimes using potatoes instead of turnips. Large beets were used in England. These were placed in windows and doorways to cast off Jack and other frightening spirits.

When immigrants from Europe arrived on the shores of the United States they brought their traditions with them, especially when they came in large numbers, as the Irish did during the 1800s. All Hallows' Eve, later Halloween, gained popularity in the United States as these Irish immigrants popularized its customs. While in Ireland people traditionally carved turnips, placed lit candles inside, and set them in windows or outside their houses, in the United States pumpkins were used. Pumpkins were relatively unknown to the Europeans, but were very important as a means of sustenance in the Americas, and thus they became part of the new tradition.

Check out some cool ways to carve a pumpkin.

TEXT-DEPENDENT QUESTIONS

1: Who were the Celts?

2: Why did Feralia take place in February?

3: Where did the jack-o'-lantern custom originate?

RESEARCH PROJECTS

1: Research an element of Celtic culture such as art, religion, or language. Find out information about this cultural element and write a brief report. Include some ways that Celtic culture has influenced the world.

2: Research a Roman god or goddess. Write a brief biography of the subject, including the origin of their name, their religious function, and other details.

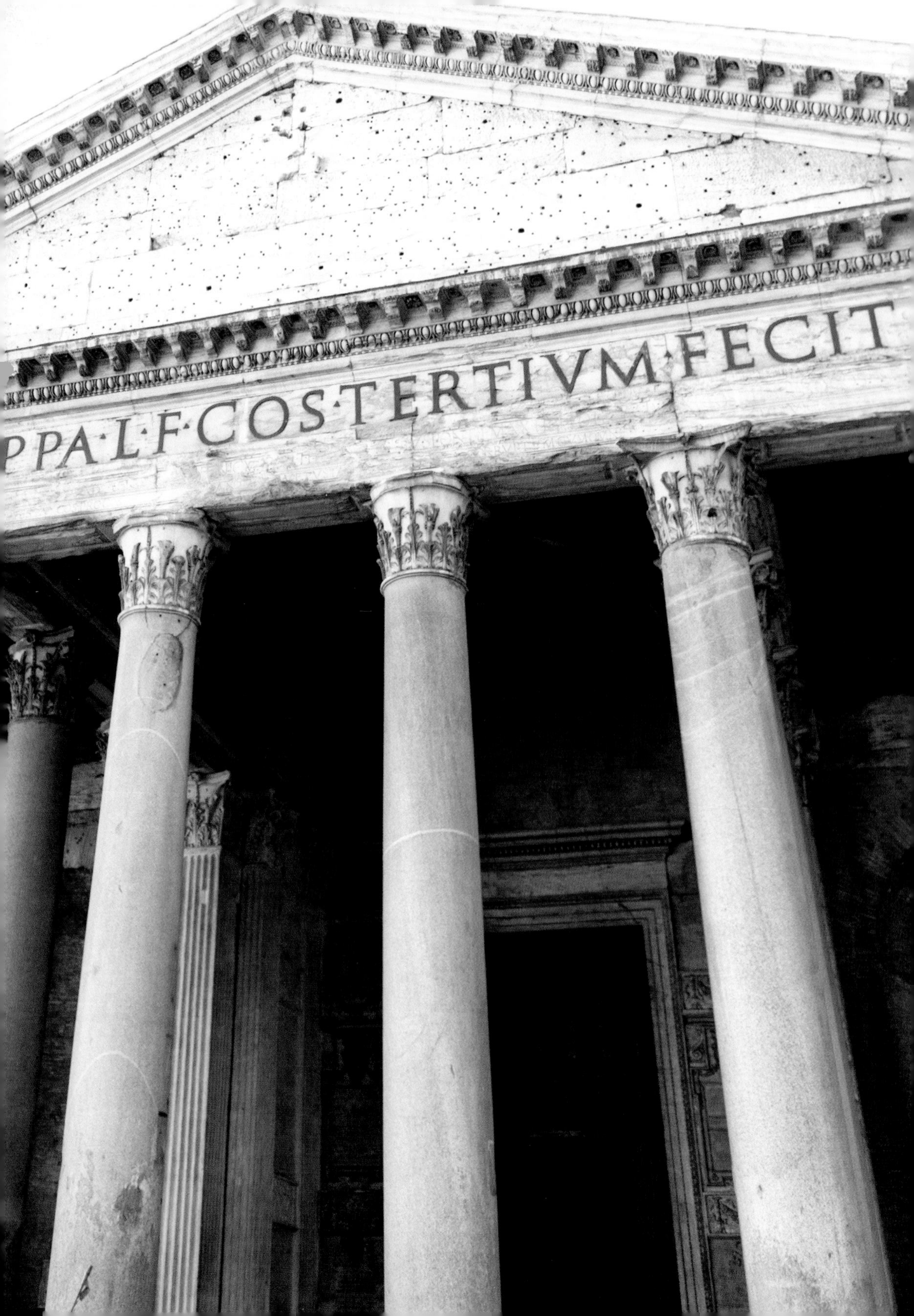
PPA·L·F·COS·TERTIVM·FECIT

2

Origins and Celebrations of All Saints' and All Souls' Days

A ll Saints' Day is a widely celebrated Christian feast that pays tribute to all Christian saints, both renowned and obscure. Traditionally, the Church designates as saints select people whose actions in life proved especially inspirational and pious. They are said to have led holy lives. The word *saint* comes from the Latin word *Sanctus,* which means "holy." Many of the major saints have their own feast days while lesser-known saints do not. Feast days are holy days during the Christian calendar when the devout are expected to honor the most important saints. But just in case they miss a particular saint's day, they have a chance to catch up. Pope Urban IV, who served as pope (the leader

WORDS TO UNDERSTAND

Anglican: Of or affiliated with the Church of England.

Clergy: People in leadership positions in a religion.

Incense: Aromatic substance burned for the sweet smell it produces, often used in religious ceremonies.

◀ The Pantheon in Rome, which survives almost completely intact, was a temple dedicated to all of the Roman Gods that later became a Christian church dedicated to all of the Christian martyrs and saints.

of the Catholic Church) from 1261 to 1264, decreed that as long as Roman Catholics observed All Saints' Day, they would be forgiven any failure to observe the feast days of specific saints.

In the Western Churches (especially Lutheran, **Anglican**, and Roman Catholic) this festival is celebrated on November 1, while the Eastern Orthodox Churches observe it on the first Sunday following Pentecost (the 50th day after Easter). Devoting time to the saints is important in many Churches because believers look to the saints as examples of how they should live their lives. All saints were once regular people who, over the course of their lives, proved to embody holiness. Because the various saints held different values and dedicated their lives to different causes, they provide believers with a multitude of different models for living a holy life.

Martyrs (people who died willingly rather than renounce or reject their faith) are also celebrated on All Saints' Day. One of the first recognized martyrs was Polycarp, who refused to renounce the Christian faith when pressured to do so by Roman soldiers. He was executed as a result of his resistance. Many saints were martyred, though it is not a requirement of sainthood.

■ Origins of All Saints' Day

THE EARLY DAYS OF CHRISTIANITY

During the very early days of Christianity, only John the Baptist and the martyrs were given the privilege of having a special day for themselves. The rest of the saints were gradually added, and they increased in number after the pope instituted a process of canonization in the fourth century.

The practice of honoring saints and martyrs of the Christian faith may have begun as early as the second century. The "Martyrdom of Polycarp," an encyclical epistle of the Church at Smyrna, written around the middle of the second century, confirms this. In the fourth century, dioceses began to exchange feasts, to transfer relics, and to partake in a common feast. Often, groups of martyrs had been persecuted on the same day; so a joint tribute seemed logical. From the persecution of the Roman emperor Diocletian (241–313), there were so many martyrs that there were not enough days in the calendar to give each one his or her own feast day. The Church, upholding the sentiment that all martyrs deserved to be honored, gradually evolved the idea of a common day for all.

THE FIRST ALL SAINTS' DAY AND ESTABLISHING THE OBSERVANCE

The first All Saints' Day has an interesting history behind it. Flavius Phocas Augustus (r. 602–610) ruled Rome and Byzantium as Eastern Roman emperor. During his reign, the Byzantines controlled the city of Rome although the pope enjoyed considerable power. Since Phocas tended to side with the popes in many of the contemporary theological controversies, he was on good terms with the papacy.

During the last year of his reign, Phocas gave the Pantheon (a magnificent edifice in Rome that housed statues of Roman gods and goddesses such as Jupiter, Venus, and Mars) to Pope Boniface IV (r. 608–615) to convert into a church; on May 13, 609, the temple was consecrated by the pope to the Virgin Mary and all the Christian martyrs. Twenty-eight cartloads of sacred bones of various martyrs and saints were believed to have been removed from the catacombs (underground burial places) and placed in a basin made of porphyry (a red Egyptian stone-like granite) beneath the main altar of the Pantheon. Boniface renamed the edifice the Church of Santa Maria ad Martyres. This church is believed to be the first pagan temple to be transformed into a Christian shrine, and its consecration the very first observance of All Saints' Day.

Historians believe that All Saints' Day began to be observed on November 1 under Pope Gregory III (731–741). During his reign Gregory dedicated a chapel in St. Peter's Church, Rome, to all the saints. Records show that over the next century, the holiday continued to be celebrated on the same date. In 837, Pope Gregory IV (r. 827–844) fixed the date of the festival on November 1 and christened the festival "Feast of All Saints."

■ Observing All Saints' Day

For Orthodox Christians, Roman Catholics, and to some extent Anglicans, All Saints' Day is a day to thank God and to honor and give thanks to the saints for fulfilling the believers' prayers. The day also provides an opportunity for believers to remember the less-familiar saints. On All Saints' Day, Christians remember such nearly forgotten saints and make appeals relevant to their specific

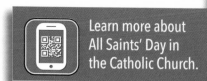

Learn more about All Saints' Day in the Catholic Church.

causes. To do so, people often make intercessory prayers. While these prayers of intercession differ greatly between religions, an intercessory prayer usually involves the act of praying on behalf of other people, rather than for oneself. The person making an intercessory prayer acts as an intermediary between God and the person or people being prayed for, thereby bridging the gap between them.

SAMHAIN AND ALL SAINTS' DAY

When the Roman Catholic Church encountered the Celtic end-of-summer celebration, Samhain (October 31), and saw that the Celts were reluctant to give it up, the Church blended Samhain with All Saints' Day (traditionally celebrated in May), which evolved into Halloween. That is why All Saints' Day has the ancillary festival of Halloween, the underlying purpose of which is to honor and remember everything that is past and gone and to begin life again.

The communion of saints is the focal point of All Saints' Day celebration. According to the catechism of the Catholic Church, the communion of saints provides "a perennial link of charity . . . between the faithful who have already reached their heavenly home, those who are atoning for their sins in purgatory and those who are still pilgrims on Earth. Between them there is too, an abundant exchange of good things." All of God's people, on Earth, heaven, and in the state of cleansing (generally referred to as purgatory) are believed to be inextricably linked in a communion. Orthodox Christians and Catholics alike are steadfast in their belief that the saints are as full of life as those living in this world. In addition, the saints are continually praying for ordinary mortals.

■ All Souls' Day

On November 2, the day after All Saints' Day, the feast of All Souls' Day is observed by Roman Catholics, as well as by some Anglicans and Lutherans. This festival originated as an early pagan celebration of the dead as pre-Christian people believed that their deceased loved ones would come back for a meal with their families. Candles were placed near the windows to guide the souls back home, and there were special places set at the table for them. Young children went from house to house asking for food for the returned deceased and gave what they received to the poor.

All Souls' Day is a day of remembrance for one's deceased loved ones. On this day, the living take time to remember and to pray for those souls who are in purgatory. According to Church teaching, purgatory is a waiting area where the souls of the deceased go immediately after death. There the souls wait to be cleansed of their sins before entering heaven and meeting God. All Souls' Day deliberately follows All Saints' Day in order to shift the focus from those in heaven to those in purgatory. It is observed with festivities and a Mass. The Feast of All Souls is a reminder of the necessity of living a pure life. According to the Catholic belief, it is imperative for

▲ On All Saints' Day a man prays at a grave decorated with candles at a cemetery in Poland.

souls in purgatory to suffer in order to be purged of their sins. All Souls' Day is a time to pray for those souls so that they can enter heaven.

Traditionally, many Europeans believed that the dead came back to the world of the living on All Saints' and All Souls' Days—including some evil spirits. Understandably, many people were afraid of such visitations. In fact, during All Saints' and All Souls' Days some people refused to leave their homes. It became customary to wear some kind of a disguise or mask before venturing outside. Not surprisingly, the people wore masks that resembled ghosts or ghouls, hoping that the real ghosts would leave them alone.

In England, Ireland, and Scotland during All Souls' Day, impoverished children and adults would go from house to house in search of food. In return for being fed, they would pray for the souls of the family's deceased. Any family that refused them food were thought to suffer bad luck as a result. This practice of going from house to house became known as *souling*.

■ Origins of All Souls' Day

FESTIVAL OF ODIN

Before it became a Church festival in 998, All Souls' Day in Europe was marked with observances from the festival of Odin, or Woden, supreme god of wisdom and war in Norse (Viking) mythology. It was believed that Odin welcomed the spirits of the brave warriors (*einherjar*) into his grand hall, Valhalla. In order to get the best warriors into Valhalla, Odin would begin wars and then send his Valkyries (the female divinities who served him) to choose the men doomed to die in battle and then deliver them to Valhalla. According to Norse mythology, the souls were gathered in preparation for fighting on the side of the gods in the final battle of the world, known as Raynarok.

▲ An Indian Christian girl lights candles of remembrance at the grave of her relative on All Souls' Day in Calcutta, India.

■ All Souls' Day Is Added to the Church Calendar

The custom of celebrating the Feast of All Souls started separately from the Feast of All Saints, celebrated the day before. The Feast of All Souls can be traced back to the seventh-century monks, who offered Mass on the day following Pentecost, for their departed community members. Records show that in the late 10th century, in a Benedictine monastery in Cluny, France, an abbot named Odilo decreed that all Clunial monasteries offer special prayers and sing the Office of the Dead on November 2, the day after All Saints' Day. The Office of the Dead was a special prayer that had been written specifically for the dead, and up until then had been mostly used by the Cluniacs and the Carthusians, who recited it during funerals. Though the author is unknown, the Office of the Dead has been attributed to many saints, including Saint Augustine, Saint Isidore, and Saint Ambrose. Among the extensive verses included in the Office of the Dead, one of the most famous lines draws from Psalm 25, reading, "Unto thee, O Lord, will I lift up my soul; my God I have put my trust in thee." Eventually this tradition took root, spread, and continued, and in the 13th century, Rome officially added the feast to the Church calendar.

In 1517 the Catholic Church divided in what is known as the Reformation. A group of reformers led by the German theologian Martin Luther advocated drastic changes within the structure of the Church. Among these was ending the granting of indulgences. According to the Church, purgatory included punishment for one's sins. The acts of goodness and piety done in one's lifetime, however, would shorten a person's time in purgatory. In addition, the Church could also grant indulgences, or pardons that would reduce or even eliminate the time in purgatory, either for oneself or a loved one. By buying an indulgence, a sinner could avoid the penalty of purgatory for sins that were confessed through the sacrament of confession and forgiven. While an indulgence did not forgive sins and was not intended to be a way to buy one's salvation, the theory behind indulgences was complicated and generally misunderstood. Because people wanted to secure their own salvation, and the Church realized that it could raise a lot of money from the sale of indulgences, the system became corrupt. Among other things, Luther disagreed with the selling of indulgences and felt that the concept of purgatory was false. Those who agreed with Luther and his fellow reformers separated from the Catholic Church and began the Protestant Church.

During the Reformation, the Anglican Church in England eradicated All Souls' Day from its feast calendar, although it has been reinstated in some churches in England, in association with what is called the Catholic revival. Among Protestants in Europe, All Souls' Day has been more stubbornly maintained. Even Martin Luther's authority was not enough to remove the tradition's observation during his lifetime and the festival's memory survives in popular customs among Lutherans.

FOOD OFFERINGS ON ALL SOULS' DAY

Because it has long been believed that on this day souls return to their worldly homes, their favorite foods are laid out on the altars.

■ Observing All Souls' Day

Today the Roman Catholic Church has specifically reserved All Souls' Day as a day to pray and honor the soul waiting in purgatory to enter heaven. Souls that have not been cleansed of sins, or those who have not repented for past transgressions, cannot enter heaven. Catholics believe, however, that the masses and prayers of the living members of the Church will help their deceased friends and families get into heaven. On All Souls' Day many Catholics attend churches, which are often draped in black. On this day family members work hard on behalf of their deceased loved ones: They can recite prayers to assist the souls on their journey as well as attend Mass in their honor. The **clergy** can also perform three requiem (*requiem* from the Latin word for "rest") masses to help the souls proceed from purgatory to heaven: one Mass dedicated to the departed, one for the family of the departed, and one for the pope.

In some Catholic homes, an altar is built for offerings of food. It is said that the dead consume the offering in spirit, while the living eat it later. The altar is often adorned with photos, mementos, and other objects that were the deceased person's favorites. Bouquets of marigolds, the flowers of the dead, supply colorful splashes of gold and orange and **incense** is widely used. A candle is lit for each departed soul.

Other rituals are somewhat less ceremonious but no less traditional. Non-Catholics, such as Lutherans and Anglicans who still observe All Souls' Day, also celebrate many of these rituals. In France, for example, custom dictates that all graves be adorned, regardless of the deceased person's religion or social standing. In Germany, as in many other parts of Europe, people bring flowers to the gravesites. In Austria, special cakes are left on the table for the dead, and the people of Brittany, in northwest France, gather by graves and sprinkle the tombstones with milk or holy water. Then they go home and leave supper on the tables for the souls. In Hungary, All Souls' Day is known as Hallottak Hapja. It is celebrated by inviting orphans into the family and supplying them with food, clothes, and toys.

TEXT-DEPENDENT QUESTIONS

1: Who fixed the date of All Saints' Day on November 1?

2: What is another name for Odin in Norse mythology?

3: What year was the Reformation?

RESEARCH PROJECTS

1: Research some of the major differences between the Lutheran, Anglican, and Catholic churches. Write a brief report comparing and contrasting the three churches, including key points of their historical backgrounds.

2: Research a figure from Norse mythology. Write a biographical sketch that includes facts about their powers, appearance, and other details.

3

Origins and Celebrations of Soul Saturdays and Day of the Dead

The Eastern Orthodox Church is most prevalent in Russia, Greece, and the countries of eastern Europe. Though the Church celebrates a general memorial for all of the saints on the first Sunday after Pentecost (or 50 days after Easter), it has several memorials throughout the year. These are known as Soul Saturdays. There are seven of these Saturdays during the liturgical year set aside especially for those deceased ancestors who would not otherwise be commemorated.

Saturday was chosen for its symbolic value, as it was the day Christ rested in the tomb before rising on Easter Sunday. Most of these days have a specific set of hymns, sung during a memorial service known as a Panikhida. A special dish called *koliva*, a

WORDS TO UNDERSTAND

Angelitos: Spanish word for "little angels"; the spirits of the dead children who come back to Earth during Mexico's Day of the Dead.

Aztecs: Indigenous people who lived in Mexico before the arrival of the Spanish.

Calacas: The decorated skeletons used in Mexico's Day of the Dead.

◀ A reveler is costumed for Day of the Dead celebrations in Mexico City.

mixture of wheat berries and honey, is consumed on these days. The combination of the grain and the honey is said to be a reminder of the integral nature of death and life, or of how dead grain nourishes the ground to bring forth living food.

One of the most important Soul Saturdays does not, ironically, fall on a Saturday at all. This is the Eastern Orthodox holiday known as Radonitsa, which means "Day of Rejoicing." It takes place eight or nine days after Easter and is a day to remember one's departed ancestors. Unlike the other Soul Saturdays, Radonitsa incorporates a visit to gravesites or cemeteries. This tradition stems back to the ancient Slavic practice of visiting the graves of one's ancestors and feasting with them after Easter. Over time, this practice was incorporated into the Russian Orthodox Church where it is maintained to this day, as well as in Orthodox Churches across eastern Europe and Greece.

■ Day of the Dead

Day of the Dead (also known as Día de los Muertos) is a Latin American festival celebrated mostly in Mexico, where it is a national holiday. Day of the Dead is actually two days of the Dead: November 1 and 2. While there are similarities between the traditions of Day of the Dead and All Saints' Day and All Souls' Day, including when they are celebrated, Day of the Dead is a festive occasion rather than a somber one. November 1 is set aside specifically to remember the souls of children who have died prematurely and is known informally as "Día de los **Angelitos**" (day of the little angels). November 2 is dedicated to honoring the memories of adults. Tradition holds that on these days the souls can come back to partake in the family's celebrations, so the Day of the Dead is a time when spirits of the dead return to enjoy a visit with family and friends.

■ Origins of Day of the Dead

The **Aztecs**, indigenous people of Mexico, customarily set aside two months during their calendar year to honor the dead. They reserved the ninth month for honoring the children from their community who had died during the year, and in the 10th month a grand feast was held for the adults who had died. The Aztecs believed a person's soul had to travel through nine stages before arriving at the final destination, Mictlan–the place of the dead. They also believed that the fate of people's souls depended on how they died (which also determined the region to which their soul would go), rather than the quality of the lives they had led. After arriving at their specific destination, the souls either awaited transformation or lingered, waiting for their next destiny.

The Spanish conquest of 1521 resulted in a blending of Aztec and Catholic beliefs. After the arrival of the Spaniards, Catholic rituals began to fuse with the existing indigenous Aztec beliefs. The Aztecs honored the dead for the entire ninth month of Miccaihuitontli, or what today would be July and part of August. It was an elaborate, colorful ceremony, with people wearing woven garlands of flowers, playing and dancing to music, and leaving copious amounts of food such as chocolate, fruit, and seeds at gravesites as offerings. The Aztecs also kept skulls and displayed them as sacred objects. The Catholic priests who arrived in Mexico and witnessed these joyous festivities were horrified at their lack of solemnity and what they perceived as mockery of death. They shortened the festival to two days and aligned the days with their own All Saints' and All Souls' Days. Though

▲ A woman places an offering of food on the graves of her brothers in Tzintzuntzan, Mexico. As part of Día de los Muertos, or Day of the Dead, many Mexicans spend the night keeping vigil over the graves of deceased loved ones.

the Catholic priests succeeded in shortening the length of the festivities, they could not tone down the exuberance of the Aztecs or their jovial attitude toward death. This was especially true in rural areas. Despite centuries of Catholic oversight and cultural fusion, today the Day of the Dead remains rooted in its Aztec traditions.

Watch how to make crafts for Day of the Dead.

■ Celebrating Day of the Dead

Preparations for Day of the Dead actually take place all year long. Families, regardless of their finances, go to great lengths to build elaborate altars, known as *ofrendas*, or places of offering, to tempt the souls to return to the places they loved. These altars are very colorful, adorned with pictures of the deceased and of objects that were meaningful to him or her. In addition, the altar should always include four natural elements: earth, wind, water, and fire. Earth is usually represented by some kind of crop, wind by a tissue-paper banner, water by a bowlful of the liquid, and fire by a lit candle. Skeletons (*calacas*), either ceramic or made of paper, are decorated to represent the profession of the deceased and hung nearby. In addition to the *calacas*, illustrations of skeletons in elegant clothing known as *catrinas* are very popular during the holiday. Mexican printmaker José Guadalupe Posada created the image of the *catrina* in the early 20th century as a means of showing that the wealthy and fashionable were still susceptible to death. The image of the *catrina* fell out of favor during his lifetime but was revived in the 1930s. Today it remains one of the most enduring symbols of the Day of the Dead.

A SOUVENIR FOR GOOD LUCK

In some parts of Mexico custom says that if a family member keeps an object that belonged to the deceased, such as earrings, a ring, or a watch, the family member will be blessed with good luck. Others take this tradition a little further and have the name of the deceased, or a picture of their loved one, tattooed somewhere on their body. This custom has followed to North America, particularly in large urban centers, such as New York, where many Mexican immigrants congregate. Honoring the deceased through tattooing is an especially popular practice among young people.

▲ People visit the graves of their loved ones at La Caleta cemetery on the Day of the Dead in Santo Domingo, Dominican Republic.

Long before sunrise the cemeteries are filled with people cleaning graves and tidying up the area around them. Candles are placed throughout the cemeteries. As in Europe, marigolds are the flowers used for decoration on this day because their scent is believed strong enough to entice the souls back to those who love them. It is not unusual to see toys on the grave of small children, or liquor and cigarettes on those of adults.

In some villages, family members or friends spend the whole night in the cemetery. Whereas some cultures might see this as a creepy, spooky observance, for the Mexicans, it is a celebration. By playing their dead loved ones' favorite music, eating their favorite foods, and remembering them with fondness, friends and family feel a sense of closeness to those they have lost. It is also a way of sharing their loss. Instead of mourning in isolation, they are able to connect with others who have experienced similar feelings.

▲ Skulls made of sugar are popular during Day of the Dead celebrations.

Day of the Dead food is often shaped in the symbols of death. Children enjoy hearse-shaped chocolates, candy skulls and coffins, and funeral wreaths made of sugar. Also popular is *pan de muertos,* or bread of the dead. This is an eggy bread made of flour, butter, sugar, eggs, orange peel, and yeast. It is decorated with strips of dough to make it look like bones.

 TEXT-DEPENDENT QUESTIONS

1: What are the ingredients of *koliva*?

2: Who were the Aztecs?

3: What flowers are used to decorate graves on Day of the Dead?

RESEARCH PROJECTS

1: Research elements of the Panikhida service, including types of prayers, locations, the role of the priest, and other details. Draft a brief outline of the service with details on each of these elements.

2: Research the life and work of José Guadalupe Posada. Write a brief biography that includes facts about his origins, influence, and best-known works.

▲ Skeletons of all shapes and sizes rule the day during Mexico's Day of the Dead.

Origins and Celebrations of Tomb Sweeping Day and Ghost Festival

Qing Ming, also known as Tomb Sweeping Day, Grave Sweeping Day, or Ancestor Worshipping Day, is celebrated by Chinese Buddhists, Daoists, and believers of folk religion. Tomb Sweeping Day is a traditional Asian festival held on April 4 or 5, the 106th day after the winter solstice (or 15th day after the spring equinox), to honor the dead. The name *Qing Ming* means "pure brightness" or "clear and bright" as traditionally the Tomb Sweeping Day observances were held at the same time that the beginning of spring was celebrated. On this day families visit the graves of their ancestors and relatives. They carry incense sticks and offerings and prepare special food. Some people carry willow branches with them or hang them on the sides of their front doors to help

WORDS TO UNDERSTAND

Buddha: Spiritual teacher from ancient India on whose teachings Buddhism is founded.

Clairvoyant: Capable of gaining information by using senses other than ordinary ones.

Fast: To abstain from food and drink, often for religious purposes.

◀ The yin and yang symbol, shown here in the center, incorporates the most essential pairing of opposites in Daoism.

rid them of evil spirits, since Tomb Sweeping Day is one of the days that ghosts and spirits roam the Earth freely.

◼ Origins of Tomb Sweeping Day

THE LEGEND OF JIE ZITUI

The holiday's origins date back to the death of a man named Jie Zitui. He lived in China in the Spring and Autumn Period (770–476 B.C.E.) and was servant to a man named Lord Chong'er. Because his crown was in jeopardy, Lord Chong'er was forced to go into exile. He found himself in grave danger, as well as facing starvation. Seeing Lord Chong'er's hunger, Jie removed a piece of flesh from his own leg and fed it to his lord, thus saving his life. After 19 years Lord Chong'er returned to his land, but he had forgotten about Jie and his sacrifice. When Lord Chong'er finally remembered, he was horrified at his lapse and became determined to reward Jie. By then, however, Jie was nowhere to be found.

Eventually Lord Chong'er learned that Jie was living somewhere on a mountain with his mother, where it would be impossible to find him. Lord Chong'er refused to accept defeat, however, and gave orders to set the mountain on fire, thinking that Jie and his mother would emerge from the forest. Instead, Jie and his mother died in the flames. Jie became a "wandering spirit" after he died. To commemorate Jie and his sacrifice, Lord Chong'er declared that the day Jie died would be known as Hanshi (Cold Food) Festival, a day when only cold food could be eaten. The second year after the fire, when the lord returned to the mountain to offer sacrifice for Jie, he noticed that willows had sprouted from the charred soil. Seeing this sign of new life, he declared that the day after Hanshi Festival would be known as Tomb Sweeping Festival or "Clear and Bright" Festival. Eventually the Hanshi and the Tomb Sweeping festivals merged.

THE ROLE OF BUDDHISM AND DAOISM IN TOMB SWEEPING FESTIVAL

The majority of the Chinese people follow the religions of Buddhism or Daoism or both. However, many followers of these religions consider them philosophies, or spiritual and moral ways of living one's life, rather than religions because they do not teach the idea of a divine creator. Buddhism is based on the teachings of its founder, Siddhartha Gautama (ca. 560–480 B.C.E.). However, all forms of Buddhism acknowledge the possibility of more than one buddha ("awakened" or "enlightened"), so Siddhartha Gautama is sometimes called **Buddha** Gautama to set him apart from the others.

Buddha Gautama believed that, through meditation, he had found the answers to suffering and how to achieve a permanent release from it. He spread his knowledge so that others could also free themselves from life's burdens and suffering. There are many varieties of Buddhism, and for most there is a great emphasis on discipline and technique in mastering perceptions, thoughts, and even the body. The different schools of thought share in recognizing the principle, as Buddha Gautama taught, that each person is responsible for his or her own enlightenment. Buddhists who celebrate Tomb Sweeping Day do so to help the souls of their departed loved ones attain enlightenment. Through prayer, care of graves, and good deeds, the living may bring the dead to states of greater happiness.

Daoism is often defined as a set of universal beliefs. One fundamental belief of Daoism is that the world is composed of opposites such as strong and weak, up and down, and open and shut. One cannot exist without the other; for example light has little meaning without darkness. The most essential pair of opposites is yin and yang. According to the Chinese, yin (Moon) is a creative force, associated with attributes such as feminine, cold, receptive, and dark, whereas yang (Sun) is a dynamic force whose attributes include masculine, heat, active, and light.

The book *Daodejing* attempts to put Daoist beliefs in written form, and is therefore considered an essential text for understanding Daoism. *Daodejing* is a short book of 81 texts or verses, believed to have been authored by a Chinese scholar from the sixth century B.C.E. named Laozi (Lao Tsu). Daoism teaches that people's bodies, minds, and the world around them are capable of deep change and transformation. In Chinese the word *dao* means "the way." Simply put, the way is understood to mean the way of nature. Daoists see the cycles of nature and the constant change in the natural world as earthly signs of a great and universal force. They call this unseen force Dao. For Daoists, Tomb Sweeping Day is an opportunity to renew one's understanding of the interconnectedness between death and life, past and present, and the flowing continuity of generations.

CONFUCIANISM AND TOMB SWEEPING FESTIVAL

Confucianism is more of a major system of thought than a religion. It was developed from the teachings of Confucius (Kung fu-tze) who was born in 551 B.C.E. Although poor, Confucius managed to receive a good education. He lived in a turbulent time of Chinese history—the second half of the Zhou dynasty. The Zhou had conquered the Shang and ruled China for close to 800 years (1050–256 B.C.E.). It was a time of social chaos and moral uncertainty, when traditional values were often disregarded or cast aside. A thinker and an educator, Confucius became a teacher in his later life and attracted many followers. His teachings have had a tremendous influence on China's civilization, the people's lives, their patterns of living, social values, standards for training government officials, and the development of Chinese political theories and institutions.

Confucius stressed the ways people can live together cordially and develop a just and systematic society. According to Confucius, the "higher good" does not come from the privileges of birth but from the practice of moderate, beneficial, and generous behavior and of service to others. Attainment comes through education and formal behavior. Confucianism does not favor military solutions, but rather spiritual patience. It does not require religious edifices or clergy, and the only sin is a breach of the rule of goodness toward one's parents, one's superior, one's homeland, one's chief of state, or one's sons and daughters. The heart of Confucianism is reformist, idealistic, and spiritual. It stresses family interaction: Members are expected to treat one another with love, respect, and attention to the needs of all.

The respect for one's ancestors was of great importance to followers of Confucius. Every home, from the emperor's palace to the smallest peasant cottage, had a space set aside for an ancestral shrine where wooden tablets bearing the names of relatives, including even remote ancestors, were kept. At specific times, offerings of fruit, wine, and cooked meats were placed before these tablets, where the people believed the spirits of their relations temporarily rested.

HUNGRY GHOST

Some people die with no descendants to remember them or to pray for them. Other departed may be forgotten by descendants who no longer observe the practices of ancestor worship. The souls of these neglected dead people become hungry ghosts, which can be very disruptive to the family. Some disruptions might be as minor as overturned furniture or cracked pottery, but other hungry ghosts have been known to possess individuals, causing mental and physical illnesses. Tomb Sweeping Day was established to pray and to make offerings for all souls, particularly those without family. If the souls of the deceased ancestors are content they do not become angry at the living. Because followers believe that the dead ancestors exist in other realms and can see what is happening in the lives of those left behind, the living take this opportunity to ask for help and favors from the other side. If the departed souls are in a good mood, they might comply.

FILIAL PIETY AND HUNGRY GHOSTS

While the Tomb Sweeping festival had its start because of Jie Zitui's loyalty, it continued because of the Chinese people's respect for their ancestors and the high value they placed on filial piety. Filial piety means honoring elders—parents, grandparents, great grandparents—whether they are alive or

▲ A woman places prays at the tomb of a relative at a cemetery in Thailand on Tomb Sweeping Day.

dead. If alive, they must be shown respect. If dead, the respect and honor should continue as if they were alive. Traditionally, many believe that the souls of the ancestors continue to look after their families even after they are gone. Because of this, families on the living side have to keep the souls happy to ensure prosperity and good health. If these souls are neglected, they turn into hungry ghosts called *gui* who unleash havoc on the living. Asian cultural practice calls for performing certain ceremonies in order to ensure for them a pleasant and restful afterlife.

Although Tomb Sweeping Day became the day to worship the ancestors, sacrifices in their honor were made on many other days as well, and ceremonies might be a monthly, if not weekly event. Families spent a lot of money on these rituals. In the opinion of Emperor Xuanzong of the Tang Dynasty (618-907) families were spending too much. In 732, Emperor Xuanzong declared that Tomb Sweeping Festival would be the official day on which ancestors would be remembered and honored.

▲ Chinese burn fake money as an offering to the dead, during Tomb Sweeping Day observances in China.

■ Observing Tomb Sweeping Day

Although the basic rituals for the day vary from family to family, they are similar everywhere the holiday takes place. First, relatives head to the cemetery to sweep and clean the graves and pull up any grass and weeds that have grown there. If there is any damage to the gravesite, this is the time to fix it. Sometimes new decorations are added to the marble as well. Then family members light incense, pray, and offer tears to the god that protects the grave. Some may **fast** that day.

The custom of *yanchi* is also followed. *Yanchi*, or "securing paper" to the grave tells the spirit that its descendants have been there. During Tomb Sweeping Day paper offerings are placed on graves. These paper offerings are then burned as a way of giving them to the dead. Following this, families leave food on the grave as an offering to the dead. The food is usually bland, if it is cooked at all. Beyond discouraging people from stealing it, this is done in the belief that the deceased prefer unappealing concoctions rather than the sweet, savory foods of the living.

Most cemeteries are located away from city centers, and families have to make a special pilgrimage in order to partake in the day's observances. Because the festival takes place in the spring when the weather is warm, families often go to the hills for a picnic after the ritual cleaning and ancestor worship. There they fly multicolored kites shaped like frogs, crabs, boats, or figures from Chinese opera.

YELLOW RIBBONS

On the morning of Tomb Sweeping Day families place yellow ribbons at the graves to keep away malevolent spirits of the deceased who were neglected by their descendants or who died in a manner that made recovery of their bodies for proper burial impossible.

When they are finished at the gravesites, families return home where delicacies are waiting for them on semicircular altars set up especially for the occasion. Traditional offerings include special items such as roast pig, steamed chicken, and fruit, along with wine and tea, as well as sweet pastries known as grave cakes. There are three kinds of grave cakes: *hong gui* cakes, *fa* cakes, and *shu zhu*

▲ Green dumplings, made from sticky rice and plant juice, are a traditional food for Tomb Sweeping Day in China.

cakes, also known as *ze gu* cakes. *Hong gui* cakes are made of rice dough that has been dyed red and stamped with a peach or tortoise mold. They are full of red bean paste or peanut powder and are the most popular of the grave cakes. For *fa* cakes the cook squeezes the water from rice milk and mixes it with baking powder, then forms cakes that must be steamed for several hours. The baking powder is included to make the cakes rise, which symbolizes increasing wealth. *Shu zhu* cakes can be sweet or salty and have herbs in them. They are used as offerings. Tomb Sweeping Day is a day that is both sad and happy, and reminds participants of the continuous cycles of life and death.

■ Ghost Festival

Celebrated throughout Eastern Asia the Ghost Festival, also known as Festival of Hungry Ghosts, is a Buddhist and Daoist festival thought to date back to the sixth century. The festival itself takes place on the 15th night of the seventh lunar month, or the month of August in the Western calendar. A lunar month is described as the period of time between either two full Moons or two new Moons. This period is called the *synodic month,* and it lasts usually 29 days, 12 hours, and 44 minutes. Although the festival takes place on the 15th night, it is believed that souls roam the Earth for the entire seventh month, which is known as Ghost Month or Hungry Ghost Month.

During Hungry Ghost Month followers believe that the gates of hell open and all ghosts and spirits are allowed to leave that realm and walk the Earth in search of food and drink. Unlike many Western traditions, in the Asian religions hell is not a place of terrible fire populated by demons, but a realm called Ti Yu that consists of different "rooms" or waiting areas where souls go according to the sins they have committed while on Earth. There they wait to atone for their sins, and as they do so they move from stage to stage of existence.

Unlike Tomb Sweeping Day, when families plan activities around their visits to cemeteries and the worshipping that mostly takes place at the gravesites, during Ghost Festival it is the ghosts and the spirits who leave their place, roam the streets, and visit their families in search of sustenance.

■ Origins of Ghost Festival

Historians agree that Ghost Festival has its roots in folk stories that emerged from various traditions, including Buddhism's festival of Ullambana, or the Festival of Deliverance. In time, Ullambana and the ancient Chinese folk stories about hungry ghosts merged and one story emerged. The story of Ullambana has its origin in India, but by the time it reached China, it had evolved to embody the Chinese traditions and the popular characters of Chinese mythology. In it, Maudgalyayana, one of Buddha's disciples, has **clairvoyant** powers that allow him to see what happened to his parents after their death. His father moved on to the heavenly realm, but his mother, who had been greedy and dishonest in her lifetime, moved to the lower realm and was transformed into a hungry ghost.

Hungry ghosts had fat stomachs and were always hungry, but were cursed with thin throats that could not tolerate food. Maudgalyayana wanted to help his mother and asked the Buddha for assistance. The Buddha instructed him to do several things. First, Maudgalyayana had to place food on a plate for the *pretas*, the most extreme type of hungry ghost. While alive, the *pretas* had been greedy and selfish, always yearning for what they could not have and more of what they already had. In the spiritual realm they had been transformed into distorted forms of what they used to be, with skinny throats and stomachs distended from the hunger. Sometimes they moved around in the company of demons. Maudgalyayana's offerings of food would alleviate their suffering, even if only for a while.

Next, he had to whisper a mantra seven times, snap his fingers, and then tip the food over onto clean ground. If he did this, his mother would become a dog and be given a good owner to care for her. However, Maudgalyayana wanted his mother back in human form. He once again

▲ Paper lanterns at a market during the Keelung Mid-Summer Ghost Festival in Taiwan. Releasing paper boats and lanterns on water are thought to please the spirits of the dead.

asked the Buddha for assistance. The Buddha declared that on the 15th day of the seventh month on the lunar calendar, Maudgalyayana was to sacrifice food and water and offer 500 *hikkhus,* or pieces of incense. Through these offerings his mother would be reborn as a human.

■ Observing Ghost Festival

Today, the offerings made and rituals conducted during Ghost Festival maintain their ancient focus on appeasing ancestors. Elaborate food is prepared. Plates and seats at the table are left empty where the dead used to sit, not only to remember them as if they were alive but also to keep them happy. Having been hungry and thirsty for so long in the lower realm, the spirits look forward to good food and drink and will seek revenge if they do not find them. Bad luck will also fall on

Get a firsthand look at some Ghost Festival traditions.

the families who fail to pay tribute to the dead properly. This practice is repeated in Buddhist temples, where altars and chairs are set up for priests and practitioners alike. Various foods donated by local people are placed on the altar such as pig, sheep, chicken, rice, and peaches. Special prayers are said over these offerings, in addition to the incantations of songs and solemn chanting.

One of the common customs is to build small fires and to burn paper money to honor the dead. The paper money, or "ghost money," is often called bank money, but is more commonly referred to as hell bank notes. These notes are burned for several reasons: Symbolically, the money, which is printed in large amounts, is sent to the dead ancestors to secure a good afterlife. People believe that once burned, the money is free for the spirits' use. It is thought that the dead will spend the money on luxuries that will make the afterlife more bearable. In addition, the hell bank notes are often burned to honor the King of Hell and to make sure that the loved ones' stay in that realm is shorter than anticipated. During the night, families burn incense in front of their

BEWARE OF SWIMMING

According to legend, horrible luck will befall all those who go swimming during Ghost Month. The Chinese believe that the angry, vengeful ghosts will grab people by the feet and pull them down if they catch anybody anywhere near the water.

household, every family competing to see who can burn more. The streets are left empty to allow the spirits and ghosts to roam freely. Lanterns and paper boats are released on the rivers, the belief being that the light on the water will show the lost souls their way back home.

According to tradition, it is dangerous to travel, marry, have a baby, move into a new house, or be buried during this period. It is a time for the dead, not the living, and these activities should be avoided during Ghost Month if possible.

 ## TEXT-DEPENDENT QUESTIONS

1: Who is the founder of Buddhism?

2: Name one of the varieties of grave cake.

3: In what lunar month does Ghost Festival take place?

 ## RESEARCH PROJECTS

1: Research the three major forms of Buddhism–Theravada, Mahayana, and Vajrayana–including their historical backgrounds, key teachings and emphases, and geographical centers. Write a brief report comparing and contrasting your findings.

2: Research some of the famous sayings of Confucius. Compile a brief selection of your favorite ones along with brief explanations of why they appealed to you and how you can apply them to your life.

Celebrating in Africa

Africa is a large continent home to many different beliefs and practices. Christian European customs and religious beliefs found their way (especially to sub-Saharan Africa) during the colonial era, while much of northern Africa is Muslim due to its long-term trade arrangement with Middle Eastern neighbors to the north. Brought by Muslim traders and Christian **missionaries** and colonizers, Christianity and Islam continue to be a strong influence in Africa. Long before those two faiths were introduced, however, Africans had been practicing their own indigenous beliefs. Finding the African people to be loyal to these indigenous traditions, the missionaries encouraged them not to drop these practices but to blend them with the customs of

WORDS TO UNDERSTAND

Appease: To soothe or bring peace to someone (often used in the sense of calming angry gods by a sacrifice or offer of food or money).

Deity: A god.

Missionaries: People sent by a church to an area to help spread a religion or perform other services.

◀ An family pays homage to their dead at a cemetery during All Saints' Day. In Côte d'Ivoire, Catholics mark All Saints' Day by visiting graveyards and laying flowers on the graves of their loved ones.

the Christian faith. One of the new Christian holidays that the missionaries introduced was the feast of All Souls' Day. Because Africans already believed in an afterlife, and the honoring of ancestors was part of most African cultures, this day was a relatively easy feast to adapt to local customs.

To this day, All Souls' Day continues to be celebrated by many Africans who follow the Roman Catholic religion. Because they believe that the spirits return to eat with the family on this day, they go to great lengths to prepare a proper meal that the ghosts will find satisfactory. As in many parts of the world where All Souls' Day is celebrated, in Africa candles are kept lit in windows to

▲ A woman washes the grave of her husband during All Saints' Day.

ensure that the spirits can find their way safely home. It is important to note that many Africans have not fully committed themselves to Catholic beliefs, however. Instead they have blended their traditional beliefs with Christian traditions and practice a new form of Christianity.

Animism and Ancestor Worship

In traditional African cultures deceased ancestors are thought to have almost supernatural powers after death and Africans believe that they can get in touch with them on an almost daily basis. The ancestors are also able to visit their descendants often, though not in their human bodies. They can, for example, exist in strange forms or take on the shape of animals. This belief that the ancestors' souls can live in other forms has given rise to animism, or the belief that plants, trees, and other things in nature, such as the sky, mountains, and rocks, have spirits or souls. Although animists believe in one Supreme Creator of the universe, they do not pray to him because he is already friendly to people. Instead, people ask the spirits for help.

While Western religious beliefs often hold the devil or other outside forces responsible for evil, many Africans believe that bad luck or misfortune occurs for personal reasons, such as the failure to please a spirit, perform a ritual, or show proper respect to an ancestor. Spirits are believed to cause both good and evil by interacting with people and with each other.

APPEASING ANCESTORS

To keep deceased ancestors happy, rituals start at the time of death. Traditionally, as soon as a person dies, the family expresses its grief by throwing ash on windows, covering mirrors, and turning any pictures to the wall. All the family members, except children and the unmarried, attend the funeral, but they are not allowed to talk during the ceremony. It is also customary to bury the corpses with objects they loved during their lifetime and that they might need in the afterlife. If the deceased ancestors do not have proper funerals, they will seek revenge on the living, much like the hungry ghosts of the Asian religions.

Because these dead ancestors have such powers, the living expect many things from them: to be healed if they become sick, to be successful in their work, to enjoy a long life with their husband or wife, and to have many grandchildren. To make sure that their ancestors are happy on the other side and can meet these expectations, they follow many practices and rituals.

Dead ancestors are also said to expect much from their descendants, particularly if the death was traumatic. They want prayers and offerings and they want to be remembered by future generations. One way the living can do this is by bestowing ancestors' names on newborns. Some Africans believe that if the dead are not sufficiently honored and remembered, they will cause disruption and abuse the living. They can become evil spirits, roaming around the place they died, and can cause illness in the living.

■ West African Vodun

The largest organized religion in coastal West Africa is known as Vodun, which means "spirit." It is practiced by more than 30 million people concentrated in the countries of Benin, Togo, and Ghana. Those who practice Vodun believe in one creator flanked by several lesser spirits who may govern anything from an entire society to an individual tree. In addition, each clan, tribe, and nation has its own spirits to whom animal sacrifices are made and songs and prayers devoted. The overall effect of the Vodun religion,

Learn more about the origins of West African Vodun.

with its multiple layers of interacting spirits, is a world where everything is holy. Even seemingly insignificant objects have tremendous meaning. Small statues or dried animal parts known as fetishes, for example, are kept for their spiritually healing capabilities.

A large part of the Vodun belief system is ancestor worship. Vodun practitioners believe the spirits of the dead live and work alongside the living. Each family is organized into a clan with its own sets of deities, or gods, that have ruled over the family since its inception. Some examples of historical deities include Sagbata, who controls the contraction and healing of disease, and Mami Wata, who lords over the movement of the waters. These gods intervene and share power with the spirits of deceased family members. The ancestral spirits occupy three different ranks of power: the original founders of the families, those who died before written history could record their names, and the known dead. Each family has a central pair of founders whose son is venerated as the ruler of all ancestral spirits. The oldest living man in the family acts as the head of the clan. He is believed to have direct access to both the ancestral spirits and the clan's hereditary gods.

■ Unique Traditions and Customs

ALL SOULS' DAY IN ANGOLA

About 38 percent of Angola's population is Roman Catholic. For this population All Souls' Day is usually celebrated on November 2, unless it falls on a Sunday, in which case it is celebrated on Monday. Three masses are conducted on All Souls' Day: one for the celebrant, one for the departed, and one for the pope. Angolans believe that the souls of the dead return on this day to have a meal with their family members. Candles are kept on the windowsills to help the dead find their way home, and an extra place is set at the table for them.

THE CULT OF ANCESTORS IN ANGOLA

Although Christianity has many adherents in Angola, many also continue to observe their traditional rituals. In Angola people believe that they move on to a new dimension after death. Referred to as the "cult of ancestors," the traditional belief is that the spirit lives on after the body is buried. Children are kept away from burial rituals. Only when their parents die are they allowed to participate.

Many Angolans believe that those who do not have a proper burial turn into harmful spirits and end up disturbing their own families, often causing diseases and death. Because the civil war in the country has claimed many lives and prevented many from having traditional burials, angry spirits are thought to roam the country. In order to avoid the harm such spirits can cause, Angolans perform other traditional rituals for their loved ones to pacify the ancestral spirits and protect the living from their wrath.

ALL SAINTS' DAY IN BENIN

On All Saints' Day devout Beninese Christians attend a special prayer service in memory of the saints and offer thanks to God for his benevolence, as well as for the gifts of the pious saints to humanity. The lives and teachings of these saints are remembered and serve as a source of inspiration to the worshippers.

TRADITIONAL DAY IN BENIN

In Vodun culture, which is widespread in Benin, death is not regarded as the end of life. Practitioners believe that the body is the shell for the life force and that after death the soul journeys back to where it came from. It is important to send the soul back to the cosmic community; otherwise,

▲ A young Vodun practitioner, possessed by spirits, dances in Ouidah, Benin.

it will wander the Earth and cause harm to the person's family. Vodun is practiced by about 50 percent of Benin's population. In many places, people belonging to other religious faiths also practice Vodun.

Celebrated on January 10, Traditional (or National Vodun) Day is unique to Benin. A festive spirit envelops the whole of Benin on this day, as singing and dancing are an integral part of the celebrations with drummers highlighting the show. Goats are also sacrificed to give thanks to the ancestral spirits.

Special festivals are organized in the city of Cotonou as well as in other parts of Benin. As Cotonou is considered the birthplace of the Vodun religion, it celebrates Traditional Day in style. Thousands of Vodun followers from all over the world flock to Cotonou to receive blessings from the head of Cotonou's Vodun practice, currently Daagbo Hounon Houna. Worshippers visit the official residence of High Priest Daagbo Hounon Houna, where lavish arrangements are made to welcome the followers. Drinks and feasting follow as people invoke the blessing of the holy spirits and pray for mercy.

DEMOCRATIC REPUBLIC OF THE CONGO

Almost half of the population in the Democratic Republic of the Congo are followers of traditional religions, which are not formalized, but encompass some common concepts, such as animism, belief in spirits, and ancestor worship. Many do not consider death a natural phenomenon. Instead, they believe that death occurs when someone invokes the power of supernatural forces by acts of sorcery or witchcraft. They also believe that the soul becomes a ghost or evil spirit and will avenge its death. Hence special rituals are practiced to pacify these spirits and protect the living from their wrath. During funerals, people wear masks because they believe that masks drive away the evil spirits. Along with the traditional African beliefs, there coexists a strong belief in the Christian God. However, funeral celebrations tend not to center on this God but rather honor elders and ancestors. When an elder dies, other elders of the tribe perform a special ceremony in his honor, and the entire village participates. It is believed that ancestors can be **appeased** by making offerings to honor them and by following and honoring the traditional way of life.

THE GA OF GHANA

Although Ghana is home to a large Christian population, many Ghanaians maintain their traditional beliefs. Many believe in a supreme **deity**, but reason that the everyday woes of human beings are too insignificant to concern this god. For day-to-day issues lesser deities, more directly concerned with human actions, are prayed to and appeased with sacrificial offerings.

The Ga believe that people should be buried in a coffin that identifies the occupation or lifestyle of the person. They also believe in an afterlife and that failure to bury the deceased with the proper rituals means that his or her spirit will haunt the living members of the family and bring death and disease. Therefore, funerals are conducted with the rites properly executed under the supervision of an experienced and elderly person who is well versed in all the burial rituals.

ALL SAINTS' DAY IN TOGO

About 29 percent of Togo's population is Christian. Along with remembering all the saints, All Saints' Day is also an occasion for prayer and remembrance of dead family members and friends in Togo. Togolese Christians attend morning services, pray, and seek blessings. Afterward people visit the graves of their deceased relatives and friends and decorate them with flowers.

ANCESTOR WORSHIP IN TOGO

Many Togolese worship the Christian or Islamic God as well as other deities, but ancestral worship is most important in everyday life. Ancestors are invoked and invited before every major ceremony.

If the cause of a loved one's death is natural, then normal burial rituals are performed. If the oracle attributes the death to evil spirits, the *babalawo*, or the highest-ranking priest, inquires whether the soul of the deceased will be subjected to more problems by the evil spirits, or whether any other member of the family faces a similar fate. If the deceased's soul is in danger, then a sheep or goat is sacrificed, and its carcass is sprinkled with palm oil and buried outside the town at a place where two or more paths meet. This ritual ensures that the evil spirits will become confused and run in different directions, not into the town or the village of the deceased.

 TEXT-DEPENDENT QUESTIONS

1: What is the largest organized religion in coastal West Africa?

2: What percentage of Angola's population is Roman Catholic?

3: What holiday is celebrated on January 10 in Benin?

RESEARCH PROJECTS

1: Research one of the African countries profiled in this chapter. Gather information about its terrain, climate, culture, and economy. Write a brief overview of the country summarizing your findings.

2: Research facts about Vodun art from both West Africa and Haiti. Write a brief introduction to the Vodun art of each region, including information about its background, key forms of expression, and other details.

◀ A Vodun priest prepares for a ritual in Benin.

Celebrating in Asia

A sia is the world's largest continent in size and holds almost three-fifths of the world's population. Many cultures and religions intermingle in this large region. While the vast majority of the population in India practices Hinduism, influencing the customs of ancestor worship in that country, many other Asian traditions of honoring ancestors come from a fusion of Buddhism, Daoism, Confucianism, and other religious teachings that have been passed down through the centuries, as well as from the cultural tradition of filial piety—especially honoring the dead.

In Asia the dead are remembered through various festivals, ceremonies, and occasions. Some are private and some are public. One custom observed in many Asian countries, such as Japan, China, and Vietnam, is the Death Anniversary. Also called Death

WORDS TO UNDERSTAND

Bhuta: In the Hindu tradition, the spirit of a dead person for whom funeral rites were performed incorrectly or not at all.

Bon-Odori: Asian folk dancing used around the Bon Festival.

Yukata: Japanese cotton kimonos worn primarily in the summer.

◀ A masked performer in a Ghost Festival parade in Thailand.

Day or Deathday, this day marks the anniversary of a person's death. Such celebrations are not confined to the date on which an individual died, but can take place throughout the year, depending on the family's needs and traditions. In both North and South Korea Death Anniversary is called Gise, and it is a somber time reserved for immediate family. In contrast, for the Vietnamese, the Death Anniversary, which is called Gio, is a celebratory occasion and a time when extended family members to get together. During these celebrations the family cooks and eats the favorite foods

▲ A man adorns a tombstone with flowers at a cemetery on the outskirts of Beijing, China, for Tomb Sweeping Day.

of the deceased on his or her behalf. They also reminisce about events that took place during his or her life. In India, death anniversaries are also observed. Called *petri pasha* ceremonies, the anniversaries of the deaths of one's mother and father are celebrated with rituals including the offering of balls of rice.

Other celebrations are more widespread and public, such as Ghost Month, celebrated in Asia on the seventh month on the lunar calendar. Ghost Month is the time of year when the ghosts and spirits from the underworld leave that realm and come back to Earth to enjoy the offerings the living have provided for them. Many rituals are involved in properly celebrating Ghost Month, such as making traditional foods, offering gifts, and burning incense; but the most important aspect of Ghost Month is the practice of ancestor worship. This custom of venerating the memory, spirit, and legacy of deceased family members varies greatly throughout the continent. For instance, on Tomb Sweeping Day, Chinese Buddhist and Daoist families visit the graves of their ancestors, clean them, and make offerings of food. The Japanese Bon Festival is a combination of large-scale, public displays of ancestor worship and private, more intimate displays of affection for the deceased. The festival culminates in a blend of the public and the private, as families congregate by nearby rivers to float paper lanterns representing their ancestors' return to the spiritual realm. Finally, Pasola is an Indonesian festival that honors the dead through jousting tournaments conducted in places where family members are believed to have fallen in battle.

■ Feeding Hungry Ghosts in Cambodia

Cambodians honor the dead during a celebration called Dak-Ben that falls on the 15th day during Ghost Festival. As is done in Japan, Cambodians offer foods and other items such as incense to the dead. These offerings are often made with the assistance of monks who are believed to deliver the gifts to the spirits. Dak-Ben is a time for prayer either at home or in a temple, depending on where the ashes of the loved ones are located. As in many other cultures, Cambodians light incense and candles to help guide the spirits home. The Cambodians also worry about appeasing hungry ghosts, and so every morning during Dak-Ben they sprinkle a rice concoction around temples and houses to feed them. According to tradition, rice is the ideal food because it is very small and can be eaten by the hungry ghosts, whose throats are too narrow for larger foods.

▲ Incense and food are laid out for the annual Festival of the Dead. The occasion brings people together at Buddhist pagodas, where they offer food, donations, and prayer to monks for the spirits of their deceased relatives.

■ Celebrating Tomb Sweeping Day in China

During Tomb Sweeping Day in Hong Kong families visit the graves of their ancestors and relatives. They carry incense sticks and paper offerings such as paper money, paper clothes, or any other paper items, which they place on the graves. The paper offerings are then burned as a way of giving them to the dead. Special food items such as roasted pig and steamed chicken, along with fruit and wine, are offered during the ceremony. Some people carry willow branches with them or hang them on the sides of their front doors to help rid them of evil spirits, since Tomb Sweeping Day is one of the days that ghosts and spirits roam the Earth freely.

▲ It is a Chinese tradition to burn paper money and gold to honor the ancestors on Tomb Sweeping Day.

Pitris in India

Ancestors have been worshiped in India since Vedic times (ca. 1500 B.C.E.). The vast majority of the population in India is Hindu. The Hindus' dead ancestors, called *pitris*, are said to reside in a heavenly realm that can be reached only after a long journey. When a person dies, the living family members have to perform an elaborate ceremony called the *preta-karma*. During this ceremony, the family presents special offerings to help the soul of the dead person (the *preta*), journey to the land of the ancestors, its ultimate destination. If this ceremony is somehow performed incorrectly, the soul becomes a wandering ghost known as **bhuta**.

▲ Devotees gather on the banks of the Ganga River in Calcutta, India, to pray for the ancestors.

Hindus honor dead parents during the *petri pasha* ceremony. This ritual takes place on the anniversary of a parent's death. Although the deceased parents are believed to be in heaven, they still need to be fed by their children. Balls of rice are often offered. Hindus believe that if they forget to honor their parents in this way, the parents will turn into hungry ghosts. The families invite Brahmans, the sages in the community who are members of the priestly Hindu caste, to the ceremony. Through them the family worships the dead parents. On this day of recollection and gratitude, family members thank the deceased parent for help and guidance and recount events from their lives.

SRADDHA

Hindu ancestors are worshipped in a ceremony called *sraddha* that can take place every year or every month. During the ritual, the family prepares and eats the deceased's favorite foods in order to give strength to the dead.

According to Hindu tradition, the ancestors expect to be worshipped. If they are not, instead of punishing the living, they punish themselves. They can refuse to move toward the realm of the ancestors and instead remain in a place of limbo. This in-between place is one of extreme heat, hunger, and sadness. The living want to avoid having their ancestors endure such a fate, so they make frequent offerings to prevent it.

■ Pasola in Indonesia

In Indonesia, during a festival called Pasola, people honor the dead by conducting mock battles in locations where ancestors have died. This is a very intense competition in which two teams of men, selected especially for the occasion, mount horses decorated with colorful ribbons and fabrics and joust at each other with wooden spears. Physical violence is a reality of the competition. Blood may be shed if a spear makes direct contact with a contestant's flesh. It is believed that the blood will nourish the soil for the upcoming agricultural season.

Originally a festival to honor only dead warriors, Pasola later evolved into a ceremony to honor all people who have died. The timing of the festival is determined by the annual appearance of sea worms (*nyale*) that come ashore to mate near the end of the rainy season in March. These worms, which live in the coral reefs, are seen as a metaphor for new life and fertility. According to tradition, during Pasola the living give new life to their ancestors by remembering them, thus continuing the cycle of birth, life, death, and being reborn into another existence. To highlight this

▲ Japanese girls wearing summer kimonos take part in a **Bon-Odori** festival, a Japanese traditional dance festival. *Bon Odori* means the dance to welcome the ancestors' souls. It is observed throughout the country in August when it is believed that the spirits of ancestors revisit their former homes.

life cycle, priests of the ancestral Indonesian religion known as Manapu may lead their followers to the ocean for a special series of prayers that culminates in the sacrifice of a black rooster to the gods.

Experience a Bon Festival in Japan.

■ Bon Festival in Japan

The Bon Festival combines traditions from early Buddhism and Japanese culture. It is a mixture of the Buddhist practice of praying for the eternal rest of the soul and Japanese folk dancing around a *yagura* (a tower erected during the festivities to house musicians), wearing Japanese costumes—such as summer kimonos known as **yukata**—and *taiko* drumming. (*Taiko* drums are large, handmade drums traditionally used for ceremonial purposes.) The festival usually takes place between August 13 and 16. In addition to its large public displays, the Bon Festival is a time when ancestral spirits are believed to revisit the homes of their families. Small household altars are constructed and food such as rice, vegetables, and sweets are offered, in addition to flower arrangements. Bon is sometimes referred to as the Festival of the Lanterns for the paper lanterns that are floated down rivers at the end of the celebration, symbolizing the return of the ancestors to the world beyond the grave.

■ Ghost Festival in Taiwan

To honor the deceased believed to live in the underworld, people in Taiwan offer scrumptious feasts on the 15th day of the lunar month. It is the custom for families

BOISTEROUS COMMEMORATIONS IN TAIWAN

While some countries commemorate their dead quietly, Taiwan does so with loud public parties as well as private ceremonies. Buddhist temples are open to the hundreds of people who go there to pray, while the streets are loud with commemorative performances, such as street marches. Businesses close for the day. At home, people prepare the deceased's favorite foods and participate in ceremonies that are not necessarily traditional but have meaning to the family. These often include burning incense or paper offerings.

▲ Boys perform the lion dance in a parade celebrating the ghost festival in Taipei, Taiwan.

to offer sacrifices of the newly harvested grain to their departed ancestors, as well as wine and freshly slaughtered pigs and sheep. It is a time when Taiwanese believe the dead return from the underworld to feast on the food provided for them by the living.

■ Tomb Sweeping Day in Taiwan

During Tomb Sweeping Day Taiwanese families visit the graves of their dead ancestors to clean and tidy the tombs. They offer prayers and food items at the graves and pray for their souls. The most common dish offered is a special type of grave cake, although it differs from one region to another. Most cemeteries are located outside towns and villages, so Taiwanese families often combine the visit to the cemetery with a family picnic, taking advantage of the fine weather and the time they can spend together.

TEXT-DEPENDENT QUESTIONS

1: What is Death Anniversary called in North and South Korea?

2: When does the Hindu *petri pasha* ceremony take place?

3: What is another name for the Bon Festival?

RESEARCH PROJECTS

1: Research the Vedic tradition, the religion that helped shape Hinduism. Find out about its origins, major texts, rituals, philosophies, and other elements. Write a brief summary of your findings, including the influence of Vedic traditions on other world religions.

2: Research taiko drumming, including its history, the materials the drums are made of, and the different performance styles throughout Japan. Write a brief report summarizing your findings, including any noteworthy taiko drummers.

7

Celebrating in Europe

hristianity is by far the largest religion in Europe. Roman Catholicism predominates in Ireland, Spain, Portugal, France, Italy, and Poland, while Protestantism is more common in England, Scotland, Wales, and the Scandinavian countries. Eastern Orthodox religions are predominant further east, in the countries spanning from Greece to Russia. Although Christians remember the dead in various ways across Europe, some customs remain the same throughout the continent. Visiting graves is seen as a duty, as is bringing flowers and taking care of the general upkeep of the gravesite. In smaller towns, families may visit gravesites several times a day during the week leading up to

WORDS TO UNDERSTAND

Colcannon: A potato dish eaten in Ireland during All Souls' Day.

Mischief Night: A holiday similar to Halloween celebrated in England on November 4.

Procession: A group of people moving forward toward a holy destination or as part of a religious ceremony.

Rosary: In Catholicism, a series of prayers dedicated to Jesus and the Virgin Mary.

◀ A gravesite adorned with flowers and candles at a Polish cemetery on All Saints' Day.

▲ Halloween-themed treats in a candy shop in Paris.

All Saints' and All Souls' Day. The entire village may gather for a Mass for the departed in the local Catholic church followed by a **procession** to the cemetery led by the priest. As the villagers reach the cemetery, they pray together and then disperse to visit the gravesites of their departed loved ones. On the Soul Saturday of Radonitsa, Eastern Orthodox Christians follow a priest and clergy to cemeteries and visit the graves of their loved ones as well.

Bells are frequently rung to celebrate the dead. On the evening before All Saints' Day, many churches toll their bells to remind people that All Souls' Day is approaching. At this time, Catholics recite prayers to the departed in purgatory and say the **rosary**. In some towns men take turns ringing the bells throughout the night.

During All Saints' Day, and often in the days leading up to it, candles are settled at the gravesites and next to the tombstones of loved ones. These are called "Lights of the Holy Souls." Because it often rains in November, these candles are covered by glass jars and lanterns. Besides taking part in the candlelight procession to the cemetery, European Catholics light candles and place them on windowsills and bureaus to light the souls' way. When All Souls' Day arrives, homes and cemeteries are aglow with the light of thousands of sparkling candles. The candles are left to burn themselves out during All Souls' Night, symbolizing life and death.

Although these more traditional expressions of All Saints' and All Souls' Days are retained throughout Europe, the Halloween customs widely celebrated in the United States have gradually been adopted over time. Costumes, door-to-door trick-or-treating, and decorations featuring images of witches, ghosts, and jack-o'-lanterns have all risen in popularity, particularly among young people.

Soul Bread in Austria

The tradition of giving to the poor during All Souls' Day is common in the countries of Europe. In the alpine section of Austria, needy children and adults go from house to house singing and praying for the repose of dead souls. In return they are given soul bread, a special type of bread baked for the occasion. This is also the time during which families distribute food to the poor that was originally made for the visiting spirits.

According to Austrian tradition, it is not easy for returning souls to find their way back home. On All Souls' Day the spirits are said to get lost and trapped in the surrounding forests, crying out to be released. But despite their crying, no one can hear them. It is up to the children in the community to wander from church to church, through the cemeteries, and to visit the nearby houses. They offer prayers and songs so that the souls might hear them and know that they have been in people's thoughts and prayers.

Mischief Night in England

The English have traditionally resisted the autumn celebrations of the dead, believing them to encourage loud and disruptive behavior in children. In recent years, however, English children have started to go trick-or-treating in costumes similar to those worn by their American counterparts. Some families have started to put up holiday decorations in their windows to let the children know that they are welcome there. Others see it as an annoyance.

Mischief Night, a festival held in western England on November 4, resembles Halloween in the United States. During this night the children are allowed to play "tricks" on the adults, including throwing eggs at cars, knocking at doors and windows, and squirting liquid detergents and soaps into gardens and front yards. Lately young adults have also started to take part in the festival, but no one has been laughing at their "tricks," which have included some serious forms of vandalism.

Radonitsa in Greece and Russia

In the Eastern Orthodox communities in Russia and Greece, Radonitsa begins with a Panikhida, or memorial service, given by the priest in the local church. He will bless foods brought by his parishioners to offer the dead. Following the service, the clergy will march in procession to various

▲ Orthodox Christians purchase flowers and light candles in observance of Radonitsa, an Orthodox Church holiday honoring the dead, held on the ninth day after Easter.

gravesites, chanting hymns and saying prayers. It is important to note that the prayers and hymns are not changed in any way for the holiday; rather, the normal, day-to-day prayers and hymns are used so that the entire focus of the service is on the memory of the deceased. As they march, the people brandish lit candles and smoldering incense while the priest holds high a cross at the front of the line. They stop together at each grave, continue chanting prayers, and observe the old custom of leaving an Easter egg atop the tomb as a symbol of life's renewal. Following the procession, the assembled may choose to return to the graves of their ancestors for further reflection, or else congregate in homes to share such traditional foods as *kuita*, a sweet grain pudding; *kulichi*, a sweet bread eaten during the Easter season; or any variety of common items such as hard-boiled eggs, pancakes, or pastries.

■ All Souls' Day Celebration in Ireland

To celebrate the beginning of the winter season, Celtic tribes slaughtered cattle and made huge bonfires out of their bones. Fire continues to be an important symbol for the Irish. In the rural areas of Ireland, huge bonfires are still lit on All Souls' Day today. Those who cannot light a bonfire light candles. As in other parts of the world, the Irish set candles on their windowsills as a way to provide light for souls who are returning home. Children have the whole week off from school and on All Souls' Day.

Colcannon is the traditional potato dish prepared for this day. It is made with mashed potatoes, kale or cabbage, butter, salt, and pepper. Traditionally, objects are hidden in the dish, such as a ring, a thimble, a small china doll, and a coin. It is said that whoever finds the ring will get married in the coming year.

▲ A man stands in front of a towering bonfire lit for Halloween in a park in Dublin, Ireland.

Halloween in Ireland

Contemporary Halloween observances in Ireland are celebrated by children who dress up in fancy costumes, visit their neighbors, and shout "trick-or-treat." Unlike children in the United States, they receive fruit and small amounts of money as well as candy. After the children return home from collecting candies from their neighbors, the entire family attends a Halloween party with friends and neighbors where a number of games are played. The most popular game is snap apple in which players try to bite a coin out of a suspended apple. Treasure hunts are also very popular. Parents hide sweets and pastries hooked to strings tied around the high branches of trees, and children are given hints as they look for them.

 Learn more about Halloween traditions in Ireland.

WARMING THE DEAD WITH THE FIRES OF THE LIVING

The Celts believed that during Samhain the barrier between their world and the otherworld became so thin that the dead were able to return and warm themselves at the fires of the living. Likewise some of the living, especially poets, could enter the otherworld through the doorways of the *sidhe*, such as that at the Hill of Tara in Ireland. (A *sidhe* was a place where the door between the world of mortals and the otherworld was always open.)

Barnbrack (a fruitcake) is traditionally eaten on Halloween in Ireland. It is usually baked with a small symbolic object inside it. One such example is a piece of rag. If someone finds it, it is predicted that his or her financial situation will be uncertain for the upcoming year. Instead of carving pumpkins, as is customary in the United States, the Irish carve turnips and place them by their front doors. They place candles behind the faces both to make them look scarier and so they will show up at night.

All Souls' Day in Poland

Many years ago a legend spread across rural Poland that on the eve of All Souls' Day, people noticed a light shining above a town's church. The priest declared that the light was the spirits of those who had died in previous years. Having left purgatory for at least a while, they had returned to the town and the people

▲ The faithful light candles at a cemetery in Warsaw, Poland, on All Saints' Day.

they loved. From then on the Poles began to leave their windows and doors ajar on All Souls' Day as a sign to the souls that they were welcome. Nowadays sheets of paper are also brought to the church and given to the priest. These sheets, called *wypominki* (naming), list names of the deceased. On All Souls' Day and some Sundays, all the names are read and prayers are recited in their honor. Farmers who have lost family members or special friends hold a memorial meal in their honor. They prepare the deceased's favorite foods and leave seats empty for the returning souls. Afterward, they give to the poor the food that was made for the spirits.

■ Candles and Heather in Sweden

In the northern reaches of Scandinavia, where winter brings a cycle of short days and long, dark nights, All Saints' and All Souls' days are as much about preparing for the change of season as commemorating the memories of the deceased. The holidays fall near the end of the agricultural season and so mark the transition between outdoor and indoor labor.

On All Saints' Day in Sweden, it is customary to take the day off work and visit the graves of deceased ancestors. Families gather to lay wreaths and jars of flowering heather, a prevalent plant in alpine climates, as well as light candles. As the many candles flicker across the graveyards, they give a sense of collective light to confront the darkness of winter. This custom was originally confined to wealthy families in larger cities. After World War II, however, the practice migrated across the country

▲ Graves in a Polish cemetery decorated for All Souls' Day.

and was adopted by Swedes of all economic backgrounds. Following the candle lighting and wreath-laying ceremonies, families gather at one another's homes to partake of such traditional winter Swedish dishes as pea soup, cured salmon, and savory pancakes stuffed with pork meat and apples.

■ All Souls' Day in Switzerland

In many places in Switzerland processions, accompanied by bands playing funeral hymns, go to the cemeteries on All Souls' Day. Families decorate the graves of relatives and light candles. The Swiss believe that the dead mingle with the living on this day so, efforts are made to make the dead feel content. During the family meal food is offered to the dead to appease them, and prayers are also said for their souls to rest in peace. All Souls' Day is a public holiday in many parts of Switzerland.

TEXT-DEPENDENT QUESTIONS

1: What is the largest religion in Europe?

2: Where is Mischief Night held?

3: What is the name of the fruitcake traditionally eaten on Halloween in Ireland?

RESEARCH PROJECTS

1: Research recipes for either colcannon or barnbrack, the traditional Irish foods of Halloween time. Compare and contrast different recipes to see if there are regional differences, alternate ways of making the dish, or other notable details. Write a brief report comparing the different recipes.

2: Select a European country not covered in this chapter and research traditions related to All Saints' Day, All Souls' Day, Halloween, or another remembrance of the dead. Pretend you are creating a new addition to this chapter, and write a short overview summarizing your findings.

8

Celebrating in Latin America and the Caribbean

A huge majority of Latin America has practiced Roman Catholicism since Spain conquered and colonized most of this diverse continent more than 500 years ago. Today approximately 70 to 80 percent of Latin Americans identify themselves as Catholics, and Latin America is the home of almost half the world's Catholic population–around half a billion people. Europeans also colonized parts of the Caribbean. This influence can still be seen today. St. Lucia, for example, is 68 percent Catholic and All Souls' Day is still observed by the majority of the island. Indigenous beliefs are also

WORDS TO UNDERSTAND

Baron Samedi: Spirit of the dead in the Vodou religion.

Fiambre: A Guatemalan cold salad prepared for that country's Day of the Dead.

Finados: Brazil's All Souls' Day, celebrated November 2.

Guédé: In Vodou, the family of the spirits.

◄ A young boy performs in a cemetery near Lima, Peru. Dancing, drinking alcohol, and eating with the deceased are part of Day of the Dead celebrations in Peru.

CARIBBEAN ALL SAINTS' DAY

On All Saints' Day many people in the Caribbean visit local cemeteries and bring flowers and candles to honor their loved ones. They clear the gravesites and set candles aglow.

observed and have sometimes blended with Christian traditions across the region. From Day of the Dead in Bolivia and Mexico, to the Vodou prayers offered to Baron Samdi in Haiti, people of this region dedicate special times of the year to honor and remember the departed.

■ Kachaypari in Bolivia

In Bolivia, several celebrations honor the dead. The Bolivian Day of the Dead is known as Kawsasqanchis. It is celebrated on November 1 and is said to be the day when the souls of the dead, called Runakuna, come back to the homes they left behind. On November 2 the souls go back to the land of the dead during a ceremony called Kachaypari, which literally means "sending off."

During Kachaypari, families stay home and cook the deceased's favorite foods. Bolivians believe that souls expect to find their families in the home they left behind, and if they do not, they will begin to whine and cause disruptions. When the food is ready, the table is set and a place is set with food for the soul. This table is the same one that families use during the "wake-meal" after the person dies. (The wake-meal usually takes place eight days after the death.) Before the family starts eating, one member offers prayers for the departed.

■ Day of Skulls in Bolivia

In the Bolivian capital city of La Paz, people celebrate what is called Día de las Ñatitas, or Day of the Skulls. A yearly event taking place on November 9, the ritual originated with the indigenous peoples who lived in the Andes Mountains. Before the Europeans arrived, it was customary to unearth the bodies of the dead three years after their death and to spend the day with their bones. Today the ritual has evolved somewhat and only the skull is used. Believing that the dead can watch over the living, some Bolivians keep the skulls of the deceased at home throughout the year.

During Día de las Ñatitas, the skulls are venerated in several ways. They are either blessed with a ceremony at the local cemetery or adorned with flowers and offerings made on their behalf. At the end of the day, the skull is placed in its resting place for another year to watch over the family.

■ All Saints' Day in Bolivia

In Bolivia, where not only every town but also every community has its own patron saint, All Saints' Day assumes a special significance. Special church services and prayer meetings are a feature of the day. For Bolivians the day is devoted to the remembrance of the dead as is done on All Souls' Day. Visiting the graves of their loved ones, Bolivians leave food, drink, and even toy boats to help the deceased in their afterlife. Candies, sweets, and bread, especially bread dolls, are customary offerings. The graves are also decorated with flowers and garlands.

■ Honoring the Dead in Brazil

In Brazil, the day to honor the dead is called **Finados**, and it falls on November 2. On this somber public holiday, Brazilians visit cemeteries and bring flowers and candles to the graves. Unlike in Mexico, where people build altars in their own homes, the Brazilians prefer to worship

▲ People visit a cemetery in Brazil to honor deceased loved ones for the Day of the Dead.

in church. Finados festivities are not as colorful as the ones for the Day of the Dead, but the underlying message is the same: People should remember and honor a loved one's life, not his or her death.

■ Day of the Dead in Guatemala

All Saints' Day, also known as Day of the Dead in Guatemala, is celebrated as All Souls' Day is in other countries. It is an important day in Guatemala. On this day people visit cemeteries, where they pay homage to their relatives and friends who have died by decorating their tombstones and

▲ Locals display large kites in the cemetery on All Saints' Day to honor the dead in Guatemala City.

graves with flowers and candles. In the village of Santiago Sacatepéquez, near Guatemala City, it is traditional for people to build large multicolored kites to fly. According to tradition, the flying of kites represents the soul's liberation from earthly confines. The kites often have notes addressed to the dead and to God attached to the strings.

After kite flying, people return home and eat special foods such as *fiambre*, a dish prepared for this day. *Fiambre* is a cold salad and in its modern version, it contains nearly 50 ingredients. Its origins can be traced to the traditions of mourners taking food to gravesites during the Day of the Dead. As the families gathered, foods were shared and mixed in a salad. Today *fiambre* can include shrimp and chicken, sausages, many varieties of cold cuts, baby corn, brussels sprouts, cheese, and various other vegetables.

■ All Saints' Day in Haiti

All Saints' Day is a public holiday in Haiti with schools, government offices, and businesses closed. Haitian families gather in cemeteries to honor their ancestors. They offer food, clothes, and other items to the departed souls. It is also traditional to trim the grass in the graveyard, whitewash the graves, and paint the cemetery fences. At twilight, people light candles and place flowers around the graves.

■ All Souls' Day, Vodou, and Loa in Haiti

Although the majority of the people in Haiti are Christian, other traditional religions also continue to be practiced. Vodou–derived from an African word meaning "spirit"–is a blend of African religions that arrived with the slave ships on the shores of Haiti and other nearby islands around 1510. Followers of the Vodou religion, much like followers of other religions, believe in a supreme being. They also believe in beings called *loa,* who, like saints, lived honorable lives. Most important, they believe that the soul continues in another form after physical death. However, their notion of an afterlife is not exactly like that of purgatory or heaven. Instead, they believe that upon death, the spirit becomes part of the surrounding world. Special ceremonies performed by the living are thought to help the spirit see and interact with those left behind in order to feel part of the community.

On All Souls' Day the Haitian spirit of the dead, **Baron Samedi**, is invoked by followers of Vodou. He is all-knowing and guards the passage between the worlds of the living and land of the Guinee–the African spiritual land where every soul goes after death. Baron Samedi is the most powerful of the **Guédé** family (spirits or guardians of matters relating to life and death, and of cemeteries) of loa. Baron Samedi's symbol is a cross (signifying the crossroads at which the spiritual and material worlds meet) and the coffin.

People visit cemeteries, bringing offerings to tombstones and asking for guidance from the dead. Many people wear lacy white robes and go around the cemetery burning handmade candles and dripping coffee and liquor on the graves. People remove their clothes, rub hot pepper juice on their bodies, and dance. Some play the drums loudly, hoping to wake up Baron Samedi. If he wakes, they will ask for favors and advice for the upcoming year. All Souls' Day is also celebrated as Confession Day, and people visit the church to confess their sins.

▲ Men and women dress up for a Day of the Dead parade in Mexico City.

Day of the Dead in Mexico

The Day of the Dead, or Día de los Muertos, is one of the major celebrations in Mexico. Although observances differ among regions, it is nearly universally celebrated in this Catholic country. The holiday is a melding of indigenous ancestor worship and the Catholic holidays of All Saints' Day on November 1 and All Souls' Day on November 2. In general, Mexicans honor dead children on November 1 and dead adults on November 2.

Experience a Day of the Dead parade in Mexico.

For weeks before the holiday, stores are filled with statues, toys, candies, and foods in the shape of skeletons, tombstones, coffins, and other death-oriented shapes. Families visit cemeteries not to grieve, but to honor the lives of their loved ones. They clean and decorate family graves and gather in cemeteries for family reunions that involve much eating and drinking and often fireworks. The Day of the Dead is celebratory rather than solemn and reflects the comfortable relationship with death that is prevalent in Mexico.

HALLOWEEN IN MEXICO

Today it is not unusual to see traditional Mexican sugar skulls set up alongside masks of popular cartoon characters. Mexican children are beginning to go from house to house trick-or-treating. As in the United States, the festivity takes place on October 31, although Mexico's Day of the Dead celebrations last two days. These new and old traditions coexist peacefully.

All Souls' Day on St. Lucia

On All Souls' Day the people of St. Lucia remember their ancestors and deceased relatives, and a vigil lamp is kept burning in homes all day long. Families also beautify cemeteries by repainting tombs and laying fresh flowers or wreaths on graves. In addition, candles are lit on the graves of ancestors as marks of respect.

▲ Day of the Dead costumes are a spectacle at parades and celebrations in Mexico.

 TEXT-DEPENDENT QUESTIONS

1: What percentage of Latin Americans identify themselves as Catholics?

2: What are the souls of the dead known as in Bolivia?

3: What is Baron Samedi's symbol?

RESEARCH PROJECTS

1: Research the musical traditions of one of the countries profiled in this chapter, including popular instruments, renowned singers or musicians, or any special songs that are played during a remembrance of the dead. Write a brief summary of your findings.

2: Research another spirit of the Guédé family of Vodou loa. Create a brief sketch of the spirit, including facts about its appearance, powers, and other characteristics.

▲ A Day of the Dead altar in Oaxaca, Mexico.

Celebrating in North America

As summer ends and the cool, crisp days of fall arrive, children throughout North America begin to look forward to Halloween. In the United States, decorations for Halloween are becoming almost as elaborate as those for Christmas. Canadians also **rigorously** celebrate the holiday with festivities including costume parties, Halloween fairs and festivals, and trick-or-treating. Throughout both countries, the holiday is a blend of old and new. In addition to the traditional jack-o'-lanterns adorning front porches and windows, modern decorations such as fake spiderwebs now appear, stretched across bushes and windows, while strings of bat-shaped lights glow in the branches of trees. Inflated ghosts and witches bob up and down on lawns, spotlighted amid clusters of imitation gravestones. People all across North America get in the spirit of the season by baking Halloween-themed cakes and cookies, watching scary movie marathons, and visiting haunted houses.

Days before October 31, children—and sometimes adults—crowd stores looking for the perfect Halloween costume. While stores stock the classic favorites—ghosts, vampires, and witches—every year they also usually feature costumes reflecting current trends, such

WORDS TO UNDERSTAND

Influx: An arrival of a large amount of people or things.
Proximity: The nearness of one thing to another.
Rigorously: Done in a strict and thorough way.

◀ Children in Halloween costumes collect candy and other treats.

as popular cartoon characters, the latest superheroes, and political figures. Many people make their own costumes out of clothes and accessories that can be found at home.

People also buy millions of miniature chocolate bars and wrapped candies to give out to trick-or-treaters. What is not allowed on most days of the year–eating large amounts of candy, playing tricks on others, and ringing people's doorbells and accepting treats from strangers– becomes acceptable on Halloween.

While it is not an official holiday anywhere in North America, Halloween is one of the most popular celebrations, especially with children. Every year nearly $7 billion is spent on candy, costumes, scary makeup, decorations for homes, and spooky music. Years ago Halloween was considered mostly a children's holiday, but today more adults are becoming involved in trick-or-treating with their children or holding Halloween parties. Often parents dress up in costume alongside their children on Halloween night, and homeowners will open up their doors dressed as a witch, a nurse, or Count Dracula.

With new immigrants entering North America and introducing their cultural beliefs and customs, traditions are blending with one another, inspiring new ways in which to honor the dead. In certain parts of the United States, such as Texas, Arizona, and California, for example, the Day of the Dead is becoming more widely celebrated, thanks to a recent **influx** of Mexicans and other Latinos from South America. It is not unusual to visit Mexican-American homes and find traditional altars built to honor the dead, alongside the typical American carved pumpkins and scarecrows. Japanese immigrants have also brought many of the traditions of the Bon Festival to their new homes in the United States and Canada.

■ Canada

BOO AT THE ZOO IN ALBERTA

The Calgary Zoo in Alberta holds its Boo at the Zoo Halloween event annually, starting the week before Halloween and ending on Halloween itself. The zoo hosts many Halloween activities from daytime Halloween-themed carnival games, and treats geared toward younger children, to nighttime activities, such as Spookies Haunted House Maze, which are geared toward older children and people who enjoy being frightened in the dark. The scariest journey of all, Walk of the Dead, is for people who want to be completely terrified.

HALLOWEEN NIGHT TRAIN RIDE IN BRITISH COLUMBIA

For almost 20 years the Halloween Night Train Ride has been running at Bear Creek Park in Surrey, British Columbia. The train runs through a dark forest full of lurking nighttime creatures. Designed to startle and scare adults, there are many characters, including characters with chainsaws, ready to pop out and frighten riders. In addition to these frightening nighttime train rides there are daytime train rides for children, along with Halloween games, crafts, and candy and pumpkin giveaways.

THE STITTSVILLE HAUNT IN OTTAWA, ONTARIO

The Stittsville Haunt began in 1998 as a small event that has grown over the years to become an elaborate and impressive annual attraction. This haunted house located in Canada's capital not only includes ghosts, screams, zombies, a dungeon with a jump-up dungeon master, a roaring and smoke-breathing dragon, and an antique hearse and coffin, but also as of 2003, it has doubled as a Food Bank drive. In 2004 the event received extensive media coverage from several newspapers and today it is attended by more than 1,000 people, and more than 1,500 pounds of non-perishable food is donated. The Stittsville Haunt is now promoted not only by newspapers but also by radio stations. Signs are donated by the local glass and sign company.

◀ The Day of the Dead is becoming more widely celebrated in the United States. The papier-mâché figures shown here are for Day of the Dead celebrations in a cemetery in Los Angeles, California.

■ United States

DAY OF THE DEAD IN ARIZONA

With its **proximity** to Mexico, it is no surprise that the state of Arizona has some of the most diversified Day of the Dead celebrations in all of the United States. Various events are held in cities and towns across the state, including mural painting, concerts of traditional Latin music, craft fairs, dance recitals, and community-created altars. In the centers of towns, such as Mesa or Guadalupe, people gather to perform traditional dances in honor of family, friends, and members of the immediate community who have died. In addition, it has become more common in recent years to dedicate dances to those who have lost their lives to war, natural disasters, or other tragedies. Another modern development is the inclusion of other cultural groups in these dance ceremonies. Native Americans, for example, have recently begun to participate in the Day of the Dead festivities. Though they perform their own dances, they still wear the traditional wooden skull masks when they perform. Following the performance the masks are placed on altars, either in private homes or in areas adjoining the town celebration. This sort of cultural exchange ensures that the Day of the Dead continues to grow throughout the state of Arizona and beyond, uniting people in a public memorial for their departed loved ones.

BON FESTIVALS IN CALIFORNIA AND HAWAII

In Hawaii and California Japanese-Americans schedule their Bon Festival celebrations during July and September, and then take part in Halloween during October. The Bon-Odori festivities often include traditional dancing around a *yagura* (the tower erected during Bon-Odori festivities) as well as bazaars and festivals that offer traditional Japanese cuisine alongside local specialties.

A GHOULISH GOOD TIME IN NEW ORLEANS, LOUISIANA

New Orleans, one of the oldest cities in the United States, is very rich in haunted history. Because of this, Halloween, often called "The Second Mardi Gras," is an ideal time to explore the city's history of Vodun, pirates, and even vampires. One of the largest parties takes place every year in Frenchmen Street, where the crowds come dressed in very elaborate costumes. But what attracts many people to New Orleans this time of the year are its cemeteries. On November 1, the city's most devout Catholics pay their respects at the graves of the departed for All

Learn more about
All Saints' Day
in New Orleans.

▲ Flowers are planted at a gravesite on All Saints' Day in the St. Louis Cemetery in New Orleans, Louisiana.

Saints' Day. The most famous cemeteries include Lafayette Cemeteries Nos. 1 and 2 in Metairie Cemetery, and St. Louis Cemeteries Nos. 1, 2, and 3. St. Louis Cemetery No. 1 is particularly noteworthy for being the final resting place of Marie Laveau.

Marie Laveau, also known as the Voodoo Queen, was a famous practitioner of Vodun in Louisiana. Born to a black Creole woman and a white plantation owner, she was born a free woman and was feared for her supposedly magical powers. These magical powers are still highly disputed today. Some people think that her magic was an infusion of Catholicism and a belief in African spirits and deities. This powerful mixture, augmented by her skill in storytelling, often convinced her followers that she possessed the ability to know things other people did not; things that she learned from communicating with spirits.

Historians, however, think that her knowledge had nothing to do with spirits, deities, or magic spells at all. Instead, because she worked as a hairdresser and made connections through her work, they believe she was able to get information about people that she used as inside knowledge. Whatever her means, people were terrified of her. That fear was further cemented on the day of her death, June 16, 1881. When the newspapers announced her demise, people were shocked, as many of them reported seeing her walking about the city during the time she was supposedly dead.

To this day, Marie Laveau remains a strong figure in New Orleans's history, particularly on Halloween. "Haunted" guided tours lead visitors through the St. Louis Cemeteries and stop in front of her resting place. There, they draw three exes on the side of the grave, hoping that Marie Laveau will hear them and grant them a wish. Ironically, historians are not even sure the site is where she was actually buried.

WITCH CITY: SALEM, MASSACHUSETTS

There is probably no place in America considered spookier than Salem, Massachusetts. Known worldwide as Witch City, it received its name because of the witchcraft hysteria that swept through the area in 1692. Inhabitants of Salem take advantage of the city's history all year long, but especially during the month of October. At this time the town is swarming with people, including actors in costume who re-create the events surrounding the witch trials. Tourist sites such as the Witch Museum and the Witch Dungeon Museum get a lot of business, and there are candlelit tours to a number of historically significant sites. The closer it gets to Halloween, the more people there are in costume—visitors going to parties, tourists joining the fun or taking part in the spook houses, and children dressing up for parades and city-sponsored activities.

Salem, being a seafaring town, had an abundance of pirates, and their histories can be found at the New England Pirate Museum. There, names like Blackbeard and Captain Kidd attract viewers and bring shivers down their spines. In addition, the Annual Official Witches Halloween Ball allows people to dress up in costume and be initiated as witches. This is an evening when the dead and the living mingle together, all in the spirit of fun.

HALLOWEEN PARADES IN ANOKA, MINNESOTA

The first Halloween parade is believed to have taken place in the city of Anoka,

HALLOWEEN CAPITAL OF THE WORLD

One of the paraders in Anoka, Minnesota in 1930 was a boy named Harold Blair. He wore a sweatshirt inscribed with the words "Halloween Capital." That was enough to attract Washington's attention. Thereafter, Anoka was proclaimed Halloween Capital of the World. Today Anoka boasts a grand parade known worldwide. On the days leading up to the actual parade, activities may include costume contests, pillow fights, fireworks, king and queen coronations, appearances, haunted houses, and face paintings.

Minnesota. When the inhabitants woke up one Halloween morning to find their windows doused with soap and their farm animals released in the town's streets, town leaders realized matters had gone too far. Something had to be done in order to allow children a fun Halloween without being destructive.

A civic leader named George Green suggested a parade as part of a larger celebration. The Anoka Commercial Club and the Anoka Kiwanis Club agreed, and a Halloween committee was created. On the evening of Halloween 1920, the first Halloween parade took place. More than a thousand costumed children marched, as well as the police and fire departments, the town's bands, the Anoka National Guard, and the Kiwanis Club. By 1930, more than 20,000 people were in attendance.

TEXT-DEPENDENT QUESTIONS

1: What Halloween event takes place in Surrey, British Columbia?

2: Who was Marie Laveau?

3: What American town is nicknamed "Witch City"?

RESEARCH PROJECTS

1: Research a festivity, celebration, or tradition for a remembrance of the dead that takes place in your home state. Pretend you are a travel guide and write a brief overview of the event for visitors, including where and when the event occurs and other important details.

2: Research Day of the Dead festivities in an American or Canadian city of your choosing. Find out how the city's residents celebrate the Day of the Dead, including special exhibits, performances, or other events. Write a brief summary of your findings.

Celebrating in Oceania

Oceania is a vast scattering of islands in the Pacific Ocean, each with its own culture. The largest and most familiar of these is Australia. Considered by **geologists** and historians to be the oldest landmass in the world, Australia was so deep in the Pacific Ocean that it went undiscovered by Europeans for many years, even when the trade routes between Asia and Europe were open and active. When the British did arrive, in the late 1700s, they found a country populated by the Aborigines. *Aborigines* means "those who were here from the beginning." No one knows how long the Aborigines had been living on the continent, though it is believed they were the first people in Australia.

WORDS TO UNDERSTAND

Ego: In this context, the part of one's personality that is conscious and tries to find a balance between desires and reality.

Geologists: Scientists who study the physical aspects of Earth.

Malanggan ceremony: A ceremony performed in Papua New Guinea to help the soul reach its destination on the other side.

◀ Australian aborigines believe the ancestral soul has a duty to return to the home it left behind to make sure that the living are taken care of.

The arrival of Europeans was disastrous for the Aborigines. Not only were they determined to colonize Aborigine land, but they also carried dangerous diseases for which the Aborigines had no immunity. Thousands of Aborigines died from exposure to illnesses such as influenza, smallpox, and malaria. Others died in battles with the settlers, which cost European lives, too. Eventually many Aborigines assimilated, adopting European customs, beliefs, and even religions, which in turn they blended with their unique traditions.

Today, Australia shows the influence of the traditions and customs of the people who have immigrated since the first European settlers arrived on its shores, as well as those of the aboriginal tribes that still remain. These tribes are believed to be direct descendants of the indigenous people who occupied Australia and the nearby islands, and they work hard to hold onto cultural beliefs that have been passed down from their ancestors. The indigenous people of Australia, as well as many other indigenous groups in Oceania, depend on oral communication for transmitting their culture from generation to generation. Storytelling, message sticks, dances, songs, and crafts are some of the forms the communication takes. As a result, historians cannot refer to writings in order to study the development of these customs.

■ Aborigines and the Dreamtime in Australia

The framework of the aboriginal belief system of the world translates into English as "the Dreaming," or "the Dreamtime." The Aborigines do not fear death because they see it as the natural time for the spirit to be released from the body back into the Dreamtime. Many of the funerary rites they perform are designed to ensure that the soul and the body separate correctly. According to aboriginal customs, a

Listen to an Aboriginal Dreamtime story.

person has more than one soul, sometimes many souls, but often just two. One is the soul they call the "**ego**," which is self-created and makes up a person's personality. The other soul is the one that comes from the creator. When a person dies, the self-created soul becomes angry. It enjoys roaming around the home and area where it lived, and it can become dangerous. This soul takes a long time to come to terms with its death, after which it finally dissolves into nothingness. The soul that was created by the creator, however, becomes an ancestral soul, which is eternal. The ancestral soul has a duty to return to the home it left behind to make sure that the living are taken care of.

Although death is accepted, this is nevertheless a time of great sorrow for the living. First, the family sits beside the grave of the deceased before burial. As they grieve, part of their purpose is to be sure that the spirit goes where it is supposed to go and does not haunt the family. The grieving is often dramatic, including wailing or inflicting harm on oneself by acts such as gashing one's forehead. Customarily leaves are burned, and the smoke from the leaves is floated over the belongings of the deceased.

Death Ceremonies in the Kiribati Islands

In the Kiribati Islands a soul is encouraged to leave the place where it lived with a ceremony called Bo-Maki. This ceremony is also believed to drive away evil spirits that wish to take over the body of the dead. The Bo-Maki is danced three days after death. In the middle of the night, all those who knew the deceased gather at the southern end of the village. They hold coconut leaves and sticks of pandunus wood in their hands. They move slowly from east to west, gently making their way north, thumping the ground and the trees. No one speaks. When everyone has gone from south to north, the dance is complete and the dancers can move on emotionally, much as the souls are expected to do after all of these ceremonies.

IT IS FORBIDDEN TO SPEAK THE NAMES OF DECEASED ABORIGINES

Speaking the name of the person who died is taboo, or forbidden, as it is considered disrespectful. People may even avoid speaking words that sound like the name of the deceased. This custom is so strong that if anyone who is living shares the same name as the deceased, that person may adopt a new name. Sometimes he or she will be called a special word that means "a person whose name is taboo." Also, the property of the person who has died will be destroyed before the end of the ceremonies, as it is believed the soul could try to attach itself to those possessions.

State of the Soul in Papua New Guinea

The belief that a person has many souls is widespread in the Oceanic countries. In the islands of Papua New Guinea it is believed that a person has three souls. Funeral rites here tend to involve not only the family, but the community as well. Community members hold a great feast and give gifts to the family in order to help the soul of the deceased move safely into the afterlife. This celebration is called a **Malanggan ceremony**.

During the Malanggan ceremony a special dance called *tatanua* is performed. First, participants sing and then they put on *tatanua* (helmetlike) masks. They then perform the special *tatanua* dance for the soul. It is imperative that once the dancers don the *tatanua* masks they remain totally silent. Malanaggans fear that, if there is too much noise, a mishap or calamity might befall them or their families. Because of this potential misfortune, strict steps are followed. It is believed that if the ceremony unfolds in a way that disappoints the dead, the ancestors will harm the living. If it is performed in a proper manner, however, then the ancestral spirits will be pleased and no harm will befall anyone in the community.

▲ Funeral rites among Papua New Guineans involve the entire community.

■ Two Souls in the Solomon Islands

Even though Christianity is widespread in the Solomon Islands, the indigenous tribes still observe traditional practices, including magic, especially in the smaller villages. In the Solomon Islands, as in Papua New Guinea and among the Australian Aborigines, the belief in two separate souls is central. At the moment of death the two separate: one goes to the land of the afterlife, which is located on either an island or in the underground and the other soul takes the shape of other forms, such as animals, fish, trees, or stones. After a person dies, the ones left behind may hope to find their loved one in reincarnated form. It is also customary for the living to search for something they would like to reincarnate into when they die. They make these wishes known to others in advance. If a person dies without such a plan for reincarnation, his or her head is placed in a wooden shark sculpture and allowed to float free in the ocean. It is believed that the soul of the deceased will reincarnate into whatever sea creature first swims by the sculpture.

 TEXT-DEPENDENT QUESTIONS

1: What does the word *aborigines* mean?

2: How many days after a death is the Bo-Maki ceremony danced?

3: Where does the Malanggan ceremony take place?

 RESEARCH PROJECTS

1: Research Australian Aboriginal culture, customs, and traditions, including art, music, rituals and ceremonies, and other elements. Write a brief synopsis of your findings, including the state of Aboriginal culture today.

2: Select a place or region of Oceania and research its geological history. Find out how it formed, notable geological features such as volcanoes, and other facts. Write a brief summary of your findings.

Series Glossary

ancestors The direct family members of one who is deceased

aristocrat A member of a high social class, the nobility, or the ruling class

atonement The act of making up for sins so that they may be forgiven

ayatollah A major religious leader, scholar, and teacher in Shii Islam; the religious leader of Iran

colonial era A period of time between the 17th to 19th century when many countries of the Americas and Africa were colonized by Europeans.

colonize To travel to and settle in a foreign land that has already been settled by groups of people. To colonize can mean to take control of the indigenous groups already in the area or to wield power over them in order to control their human and physical resources.

commemorate To honor the memory of a person or event

commercialization The act of reorganizing or reworking something in order to extract profit from it

descendant One who comes from a specific ancestor

Eastern Orthodox Church The group of Christian churches that includes the Greek Orthodox, Russian Orthodox, and several other churches led by patriarchs in Istanbul (Constantinople), Jerusalem, Antioch, and Alexandria.

effigy A representation of someone or something, often used for mockery

equinox Either of the two times during each year when night and day are approximately the same length of time. The spring equinox typically falls around March 21 and the autumnal equinox around September 23.

fast To abstain from eating for a set period of time, or to eat at only prescribed times of the day as directed by religious custom or law.

feast day A day when a religious celebration occurs and an intricate feast is prepared and eaten.

firsthand From the original source; experienced in person

Five Pillars of Islam The five duties Muslims must observe: declaring that there is only one God and Muhammad is his prophet, praying five times a day, giving to charity, fasting during Ramadan, and making a pilgrimage to Mecca

foundation myth A story that describes the foundation of a nation in a way that inspires its people

Gregorian calendar The calendar in use through most of the world

hedonism The belief that pleasure is the sole good in life

Hindu A follower of Hinduism, the dominant religion of India

imam A leader; a scholar of Islam; the head of a mosque

indigenous Originating in or native to a specific region; often refers to living things such as people, animals, and plants

Islam The religious faith of Muslims. Muslims believe that Allah is the only God, and Muhammad was his prophet

Judaism A religion that developed among the ancient Hebrews. Followers of Judaism believe in one God and follow specific laws written in the Torah and the Talmud, and revealed to them by Moses.

Julian calendar Is named after Julius Caesar, a military leader and dictator of ancient Rome, who introduced it in 46 B.C.E. The Julian calendar has 365 days divided into 12 months, and begins on January 1. An extra day, or leap day, is added every four years (February 29) so that the years will average out to 365.242, which is quite close to the actual 365.242199 days of Earth's orbit.

lower realm In the Asian tradition, the place where the souls end up if their actions on Earth were not good

lunar Related to the Moon

martyr A person who willingly undergoes pain or death because of a strong belief or principle

masquerade A party to which people wear masks, and sometimes costumes or disguises

millennium 1,000 years

monarch A king or queen; a ruler who inherits the throne from a parent or other relative

monotheism The belief in the supremacy of one god (and not many) that began with Judaism more than 4,000 years ago and also includes the major religions of Islam and Christianity.

mosque An Islamic house of worship

mourning The expression of sorrow for the loss of a loved one, typically involving

movable feast A religious feast day that occurs on a different day every year

Muhammad The prophet to whom God revealed the Quran, considered the final prophet of Islam

mullah A clergyman who is an expert on the Quran and Islamic religious matters

Muslim A person who follows the Islamic religion

New Testament The books of the Bible that were written after the birth of Christ

New World A term used to describe the Americas from the point of view of the Western Europeans (especially those from France, England, Portugal, and Spain) who colonized and settled what is today North and South America.

offering Donation of food or money given in the name of a deity or God

Old Testament The Christian term for the Hebrew Scriptures of the Bible, written before the birth of Christ

oral tradition Stories told aloud, rather than written, as a way to pass down history

pagan Originally, someone in ancient Europe who lived in the countryside; a person or group that does not believe in one god, but often believes in many gods that are closely connected to nature and the natural world

pageantry Spectacle, elaborate display

parody Imitation of something, exaggerated for comic effect—for example, a parody of science fiction movies.

patria Fatherland; nation; homeland

peasant People who farm land that usually belongs to someone else, such as a landowner

penance The repentance of sins, including confessing, expressing regret for having committed them, and doing something to earn forgiveness

piety A strong belief in and correspondingly fervent practice of religion

pilgrimage A journey undertaken to a specific destination, often for religious purposes

prank A mischievous or humorous trick

pre-Columbian Of or relating to the period before Christopher Columbus arrived in the Americas

procession A group of people moving together in the same direction, especially in a type of celebration

prophecy A prediction about a future event

prophet An individual who acts as the interpreter or conveyer of the will of God and spreads the word to the followers or possible followers of a religion. A prophet can also be a stirring leader or teacher of a religious group. Capitalized it refers to Muhammad.

Protestant A member of a Christian denomination that does not follow the rule of the pope in Rome and is not one of the Eastern Orthodox Churches. Protestant denominations include Anglicans (Episcopalians), Lutherans, Presbyterians, Methodists, Baptists, and many others.

Quran The holy book of Islam

rabbi A Jew who is ordained to lead a Jewish congregation; rabbis are traditionally teachers of Judaism.

reincarnation The belief in some religions that after a person or animal dies, his or her soul will be reborn in another person or animal; it literally means, "to be made flesh again." Many Indian religions such as Hinduism, Sikhism, and Jainism, believe in reincarnation.

repentance To express regret and ask forgiveness for doing something wrong or hurtful.

requiem A Mass for the souls of the dead, especially in the Catholic Church

revel To celebrate in a joyful manner; to take extreme pleasure

ritual A specific action or ceremony typically of religious significance

sacred Connected with God or religious purposes and deemed worthy of veneration and worship

sacrifice Something given up or offered in the name of God, a deity or an ancestor.

shaman A spiritual guide who a community believes has unique powers to tell the future and to heal the sick. Shamans can mediate or cooperate with spirits for a community's advantage. Cultures that practice shamanism are found all over the world still today.

Shia A Muslim sect that believes that Ali, Muhammad's son-in-law, should have succeeded Muhammad as the caliph of Islam; a common sect in Iran but worldwide encompassing only about 15 percent of Muslims

solar calendar A calendar that is based on the time it takes Earth to orbit once around the Sun

solar Related to the Sun

solilunar Relating to both the Sun and Moon

solstice Day of the year when the hours of daylight are longest or shortest. The solstices mark the changing of the seasons–when summer begins in the Northern Hemisphere (about June 22) and winter begins in the Northern Hemisphere (about December 22).

spiritual Of or relating to the human spirit or soul, or to religious belief

Sunni The largest Islamic sect, including about 85 percent of the world's Muslims

supernatural Existing outside the natural world

Talmud The document that encompasses the body of Jewish law and customs

Torah Jewish scriptures, the first five books of the Hebrew scriptures, which serve as the core of Jewish belief

veneration Honoring a god or a saint with specific practices

vigil A period in which a person stays awake to await some event

Vodou A religion rooted in traditional African beliefs that is practiced mostly in Haiti, although it is very popular in the West Indies as well. Outside of Haiti it is called *Vodun.*

Further Resources

■ Books

Halloween: The History of America's Darkest Holiday. By David J. Skal. Published in 2016 by Dover Publications, Mineola, NY. A cultural historian looks at the history of Halloween celebrations from Celtic origins to the present.

12 Major World Religions: The Beliefs, Rituals, and Traditions of Humanity's Most Influential Faiths. By Jason Boyett. Published in 2016 by Zephyros Press, Berkeley, CA. A guide to the world's major religions.

The Art of Coco. By Lee Unkrich. Published in 2017 by Chronicle Books, San Francisco. Companion book to the hit Disney Pixar film about the Mexican Day of the Dead culture.

The Mammoth Book of Halloween Stories: Terrifying Tales Set on the Scariest Night of the Year! By Stephen Jones. Published in 2018 by Skyhorse Publishing, New York. Collection of horror stories all set on Halloween.

America's Favorite Holidays. By Bruce David Forbes. Published in 2015 by University of California Press, Oakland, CA. Explores how five of America's culturally important holidays–Christmas, Valentine's Day, Easter, Halloween, and Thanksgiving–came to be what they are today, seasonal and religious celebrations heavily influenced by modern popular culture.

Haitian Vodou: An Introduction to Haiti's Indigenous Spiritual Tradition. By Mambo Chita Tann. Published in 2016 by Llewellyn Publications, Woodbury, MN. Exploration of the history and contemporary practices of this fascinating spiritual tradition rich with ceremonies, magic, songs, prayers, and dances.

A Season with the Witch: The Magic and Mayhem of Halloween in Salem, Massachusetts. By J. W. Ocker. Published in 2016 by Countryman Press, New York. An Edgar Award-winning travel writer spends an autumn living in one of America's spookiest tourist destinations: Salem, Massachusetts.

Buddhism (Major World Religions). By Mark Thomas. Published in 2017 by Mason Crest, Broomall, Pa. This volume is one in a series exploring the world's major religious traditions. It explores the history, beliefs, and practices of Buddhism from its founding through the present day.

■ Web Sites

Asia Source. http://www.asiasource.org. A Web site geared toward the Asian community and all those interested in Asian culture. Information on history, culture, and travel, as well as religious traditions.

Celtic Europe. http://www.watson.org/~leigh/celts.html. An extremely extensive Web site detailing the history and culture of ancient populations. Links to Celtic Culture lead to more online resources about Celtic history and lore.

Day of the Dead. http://www.dayofthedead.com. Award-winning Web site geared to those wishing to learn about Mexico's Day of the Dead. Covers the varied traditions in Mexico's towns, their history, food preparations, and poems.

The Ghost Festival. http://www.religionfacts.com/ghost-festival. An entry within the larger Web site called Religious Facts. Here, Chinese religious beliefs are covered, as well as the traditions associated with them, ways to celebrate them, and their historical contexts.

History of Halloween. http://www.history.com/topics/halloween. A link within the History Channel's Web site. A brief history of Halloween in America and across the world, as well as the origins of Halloween superstitions, haunted houses and symbols. Videos included.

Irish History. https://www.ria.ie/research-projects/irish-history-online. One of the most authoritative Web sites on Irish history online. It is associated with the Royal Irish Academy.

The New Advent. http://newadvent.org/cathen/01315a.htm. A religious online encyclopedia. Information on topics such as All Saints' Day, as well as more wide-ranging subjects such as Bible prophets, saints, and even traditional foods.

Taiwan Midsummer Ghost Festival. http://www.chinatownconnection.com/taiwan-ghost-festival.htm. Articles related to Taiwan's Ghost Festival, such as beliefs, history, and crafts related to the holiday. Additional articles on Taiwan are also available.

Index

Picture Credits